*The Freshwater Angler*™

# The Art of
# FLY TYING

John van Vliet

**Creative Publishing**
international

Chanhassen, Minnesota

JOHN VAN VLIET is the author of more than half a dozen books on fly fishing and fly tying. An accomplished fly fisherman and fly tier, he has fly fished throughout the world and is a regular contributor to the *New York Times*. He lives in Minneapolis, MN.

**Creative Publishing international**

Copyright © 2007
Creative Publishing international, Inc.
18705 Lake Drive East
Chanhassen, Minnesota 55317
1-800-328-3895
www.creativepub.com
All rights reserved

Printed in China

10 9 8 7 6 5 4 3 2 1

Library of Congress Cataloging-in-Publication Data

Van Vliet, John.
  The Art of fly tying : over 200 classic and new patterns / John van Vliet.
    p. cm.
  Includes index.
  ISBN-13: 978-1-58923-346-1 (hard cover)
  ISBN-10: 1-58923-346-8 (hard cover)
  1. Fly tying. 2. Flies, Artificial. I. Title.

SH451.V35 2007
688.7'9124--dc22                                   2007008481

*President/CEO:* Ken Fund
*Vice President Sales/Marketing:* Peter Ackroyd
*Publisher:* Winnie Prentiss
*Executive Managing Editor:* Barbara Harold
*Production Managers:* Laura Hokkanen, Linda Halls

*Creative Director:* Michele Lanci-Altomare
*Senior Design Manager:* Brad Springer
*Design Managers:* Jon Simpson, Mary Rohl
*Cover Design:* Danielle Smith
*Illustrators:* Thomas Boll, Jon Q. Wright
*Photographers:* Steve Galvin, Stuart Block, Cy DeCosse, David H. Funk, Rebecca Hawthorne, Rex Irmen, William Lidner, Mark Macemon, Paul Najlis, Charles Nields, Tony Oswals, Mike Parker
*Page 72 photo:* © Cathy & Barry Beck
*Contributors:* Michael Allison; Mike Alwin; The American Museum of Fly Fishing—Alanna Fisher; Tom Andersen; Dan Bailey's Fly Shop—Dan Bailey; Wayne Bartz; John Edstrom; Gregory P. Farley; John Goplin; Fly Fisherman Magazine—John Randolph; H. Gerstner & Sons, Chests & Cases—Jack Campbell; Dean Hansen; Paul Hanson; Mark Larson; Thomas "TL" Lauerman, Wapsi Fly; Metz Hatchery; Bob Mitchell's Fly Shop—the late Bob & Jean Mitchell; O. Mustad & Sons; J. Rex & Associates—Jim Rex; The Orvis Company—Tim Joseph, Tom Rosenbauer; Partridge of Redditch; Plano Molding Company—Bill Cork, Joe Wolf; Winnie Prentiss; Jesse Riding, Rainy's Flies; Trapper Rudd; Kris Shelton, Brookside Flies; Catherine L. Smith, Windy Hill; John Talley; Umpqua Feather Merchants—Ken Menard; Marcos Vergara, Hareline; Kevin Wible; Mark Woyak

## *The Art of Fly Tying*
**Interactive CD-ROM for Macintosh & Windows**
©2007 Creative Publishing international, Inc. and its licensors.
All rights reserved.

Contains Adobe® Flash® technology by Adobe Systems Incorporated. This "The Art of Fly Tying CD-Rom" contains Adobe® Flash® Player software by Adobe Systems Incorporated. Copyright © 1995-2006 Adobe Macromedia Software LLC. All rights reserved. Protected by U.S. Patent 6,879,327; Patents Pending in the U.S. and other countries. Adobe and Flash are trademarks of Adobe Systems Incorporated.

### SYSTEM REQUIREMENTS:
• **Macintosh**
PowerPC 500MHz or faster
128 MB RAM
Mac OS X v.10.1.x, 10.2.x, 10.3.x, or 10.4.x

• **Windows**
Intel Pentium II 450MHz or faster processor (or equivalent)
128 MB RAM
Windows 98 or higher

# Contents

# Introduction

Of all the ways to catch a fish, few are as exciting and rewarding as catching one on a fly you've tied yourself. An artificial fly can entice the slow rise of a trout or the explosive strike of a largemouth bass. And for many fly anglers, tying the fly is as satisfying as landing the fish.

For thousands of years, anglers have been wrapping hooks with wool, fur, feathers and thread in order to imitate some morsel in a fish's diet and fool the fish into taking the hook. But despite this long history, the methods and techniques of fly tying remain essentially unchanged.

Fly tying is the craft of combining several basic elements—tail, body, wing and hackle—to create a completed fly. It can be accomplished with a few simple tools and materials. And once you've learned the basics, you'll find that most fly patterns are simple and easy to tie.

The purpose of this book is to introduce you to the fundamentals of fly tying, including the tools, materials and techniques required for tying, and provide you with clear, color photographs of the most popular fly patterns and recipes you need to tie them.

The first section, "Understanding Fly Tying," gives you a brief history of fly tying and its traditions, from the earliest written descriptions to today's innovations in materials.

This section also shows you the wide variety of aquatic insects and other foods that make up a fish's diet and explains how understanding these various aquatic foods can help you tie more accurate and effective imitations.

The second section, "Fly-Tying Tools & Materials," shows you all the tools you'll need to tie flies, and the wide range of hooks, thread and materials available. You'll also learn tips on organizing your work area for more efficient tying.

"Fly-Tying Basics" includes a description of the many components of a fly, as well as a section on Saltwater Fly-Tying Basics. You'll learn about each stage of tying a fly, from how to start the thread on the hook to the best finishing knots. In between, you'll find dozens of essential techniques for tying tails, bodies, wings, hackle and other parts of a fly, with each technique shown in full-color, step-by-step photos.

The last section, "Fly Patterns," shows you how to combine these elements to create a finished fly. You'll learn step-by-step procedures for tying six different fly types, including streamers, nymphs, dry flies, wet flies, terrestrials, bass flies, and saltwater flies.

After each basic pattern, we'll show you photos and complete recipes for dozens of other patterns that can be tied using the techniques demonstrated in the initial step-by-step sequence. In all, you'll learn more than two hundred classic and new patterns.

Whether you're just starting or have been tying for years, this book is sure to expand your knowledge and improve your skills in the art of fly tying.

Made by C.F. ORVIS, Manchester, Vt.
COPYRIGHTED

Bibliotheca

ARTHUR HOWARD
EX LIBRIS
THOMPSON

# History of Fly Tying

No other aspect of modern sport-fishing is as steeped in tradition and history as tying and fishing artificial flies.

The tools and materials of fly tying are reminiscent of a time when the rewards of a season's hunt — the feathers and furs of game birds and animals — were used to create fly patterns that would catch fish.

*Many of today's popular fly patterns call for man-made materials*

While many people credit Izaak Walton and his 1676 edition of *The Compleat Angler* with the beginning of fly fishing, the origins of tying and fishing artificial flies actually date back thousands of years.

The earliest written account appeared in the third century A.D., when the writer Aelianus described a Macedonian method of catching fish using artificial flies:

> *"They do not use [natural] flies for bait, for if a man's hand touch them they lose their natural color, their wings wither, and they become unfit food for the fish.*

> *"[Instead] they fasten crimson wool around a hook, and fix on to the wool two feathers that grow under a cock's wattles, and which in color are like wax."*

Centuries later, in 1496, an Englishwoman named Dame Juliana Berners wrote the popular *Treatise of Fishing with an Angle*, which included a description of dressing a hook with virtually the same materials used by the Macedonians.

In the years between Aelianus and Berners, fishing with an artificial fly had evolved from a practical way to catch fish to a highly refined sport, but the method of winding materials onto a hook remained the same.

HUNDRED-YEAR-OLD fly patterns (left) show the high level of skill and wide range of natural materials employed by flytiers of the time.

Interest in fly tying blossomed in the 1880s, as flytiers in Europe, Britain and America were tying both gaudy, fanciful wet flies and increasingly exact imitations of natural insects. But in America, these fancy wet-fly patterns gradually gave way to the more realistic flies, as the native Eastern brook trout was slowly replaced by the brown trout.

The brown, an import from Germany in 1883, was far more selective than the brookie. As a result, flytiers were forced to create patterns that more closely resembled the natural insects that made up the trout's diet.

At about the same time, in 1881, Dr. Henshall's *Book of the Black Bass* introduced artificial flies — many of them traditional trout patterns — to countless bass fishermen.

In the 1950s, the feathers and fur of exotic and endangered species that had once been among the standard fly-tying materials became increasingly difficult to obtain. Flytiers turned to other sources of natural materials, and patterns no longer called for owl, condor or imported jungle cock feathers.

In the 1970s, the introduction of synthetics, such as Antron® and Mylar®, revolutionized fly tying. Colors, particularly fluorescents, that were unobtainable in nature or through dying natural materials, were now available in synthetic threads, dubbing and wing materials.

Today, in an age of man-made materials and high-tech equipment, when fly anglers pursue everything from bass and pike to bonefish and tarpon, the popularity of fly tying shows no sign of diminishing as another generation learns the craft of winding materials onto a hook in order to entice a fish to strike.

# Aquatic Insects & Other Foods

One of the secrets to tying effective flies is understanding the foods that fish eat. Trout, for example, rely heavily on aquatic insects for food, explaining why most trout flies resemble some stage in the life cycle of an aquatic insect.

Traditional fly patterns were designed to imitate a small number of species and stages of aquatic insects. Today, there are fly patterns imitating practically all of them, as well as minnows, frogs, leeches, sculpins, crabs, shrimp and many other kinds of aquatic foods.

The majority of fly patterns fall into the category of *imitators.* Many flytiers go to great lengths to "match the hatch," creating precise impressions of a specific stage of a certain insect species.

But some fly patterns are classified as *attractors*, because they are tied in colors and shapes that do not resemble any natural aquatic food. These patterns trigger a fish's defense mechanism or arouse its curiosity, causing it to strike the fly.

*Fly types include: (1) attractor, (2) imitator and (3) searching pattern*

Yet another category, called *searching patterns*, is used to locate fish. A searching pattern does not resemble any specific natural insect, but rather a broad range of similar insect types. These patterns are best when exploring new water.

The key to successful imitation is knowing what the natural insect looks like. Whenever possible, study the size, shape and color of insect the fish are eating. Many flytiers also observe the action and examine the texture of the insect and use materials that will duplicate them.

Following are the growth stages of the four main groups of aquatic insects: mayflies, caddisflies, midges and stoneflies.

LOOK for streamside insect activity to help you match the hatch. Clouds of emerging or mating insects (above) are an indication of what the fish may be eating. When no insects are visible above the water, turning over submerged rocks (inset) can help you select a nymph pattern.

MAYFLY life stages include the nymph; *subimago*, or dun; and *imago*, or spinner (pp. 12 - 13). All stages have two or three tail filaments. Adults (duns and spinners) have two large upright wings, and some have a set of smaller wings. The wings of mayfly duns are opaque; spinners, transparent.

CADDISFLIES have no tails and four wings, which are folded tent-style over their bodies when not in flight. The stages of the caddisfly are: larva, pupa and adult. In many species, the larva builds a shell, or case, in which to live. Adults and larvae range in color from tan and cream to olive and dark brown.

MIDGES are generally quite small, with only two wings and no tails. They are found most often in slow-moving water and vary greatly in color. Midges, like caddisflies, mature from larva to pupa to adult. The mosquito is a common type of midge.

STONEFLY nymphs and adults have two short tail filaments. Adults also have four hard, shiny wings that lie flat over the body when not in flight. Stoneflies mature from nymph to adult with no intermediate stage. Some stonefly species are among the largest aquatic insects, although others can be quite small. Many species of stonefly emerge and mate on land, not on the water, returning to the water to lay their eggs.

Blue Dun

Nymphs emerge as "duns."

Duns fly away to nearby vegetation and molt into "spinners."

Adults mate in swarms over the water.

Females deposit eggs. All adults die soon after.

Emergence stage. Nymphs begin to swim to the surface.

Rusty Spinner

Hare's Ear

Eggs sink to streambed. Cycle complete.

*BEGINNING OF NEW CYCLE*

Eggs hatch into nymphs. They live in the streambed for up to two years.

MAYFLY LIFE CYCLE. Mayfly eggs hatch into nymphs, imitated by patterns like this Hare's Ear Nymph (inset). This stage lasts from a few months up to two years, then the nymphs ascend to the surface and hatch, or *emerge*, as duns. This stage is imitated by dry-fly patterns like this Blue Dun (inset). Duns then fly up into the streamside vegetation, where they shed their skin, or *molt*, to become spinners. Mayflies mate over the water, often in swarms. Females deposit their eggs by spinning just above the surface and repeatedly dropping to the water. *Spent* mayflies, like this Trico Spinner imitation (inset), have wings that lie flat on the surface.

OTHER AQUATIC FOODS and their imitations include: amphibians, such as a (1) frog, imitated by (2) Krazy Kicker Frog; terrestrials, such as a (3) grasshopper, imitated by (4) Dave's Hopper; aquatic insects, such as a (5) stonefly nymph, imitated by (6) Black Stonefly, (7) caddisfly larva, imitated by (8) Peeking Caddis, (9) midge larva, imitated by (10) Brassie; crustaceans, such as a (11) scud, imitated by (12) Olive Scud, and a (13) crayfish, imitated by (14) Dave's Crayfish. Larger fish, particularly brown trout and smallmouth bass, feed on minnows and other baitfish, such as a (15) sculpin, imitated by (16) Muddler Minnow.

# Fly-Tying Tools

Learning to tie flies with the right tools can make the difference between success and frustration.

Although most flytiers eventually accumulate a sizable collection of tools for a variety of specialized tasks, the beginner need only be concerned with the following basic tools: a fly-tying vise; scissors; thread holder, or bobbin; hackle pliers and hair stacker. Other handy tools include a whip finisher, dubbing needle, tweezers and hackle gauge.

It's a good idea to try a number of different styles of each tool you plan to buy. Your local fly tackle dealer can help you choose equipment to fit your skills and budget.

The following pages are intended to acquaint you with just a few of the many different styles of quality tools available. Your final choice is a matter of personal preference.

# Fly-tying Vises

A good fly-tying vise should be easy to use, hold the hook securely and adjust easily to a wide range of hook sizes.

For most flytiers, a simple lever-action vise is adequate. However, for large bass and pike patterns, many tiers prefer a spring-loaded vise, which adjusts automatically to almost any size hook.

Vises come in clamp and pedestal models. Clamp models attach securely to your tying surface; the C-clamp should fit tables up to $1\frac{1}{2}$ inches thick. Pedestal models should be heavy enough to stay in one place as you tie. Because of their weight, however, they are somewhat less portable than clamp models.

POPULAR VISES include: (1) Griffen clamp-base model with screw-adjustable head and jaws, for most fly-tying tasks; (2) Dyna-King Traveler, a pedestal model with rotary head, which allows for 360-degree viewing of fly; (3) Thompson Model "A," a fixed-head vise with lever-adjustable jaws and clamp base, for all-purpose tying; (4) Orvis Premier, a rotary-style vise with adjustable head angle, which allows you to tie materials to bottom of fly without removing hook; and (5) Regal spring-loaded model, which adjusts to a wide range of hook sizes.

# Bobbins

BOBBINS and accessories include: (1) traditional open-frame bobbin for standard-size spools; (2) vertical thread holder for long spools; (3) wire-loop tool for threading bobbin; (4) multi-spool bobbin, which fits a variety of spool sizes; and (5) bobbin with smooth ceramic tube, designed to reduce snagging or cutting of thread.

The bobbin performs several important functions. It holds the spool of thread as you tie, allows you to wrap the thread onto the hook precisely where you want it, and maintains proper tension on the thread. Whenever you pause to add or trim materials, simply let the bobbin hang below the hook. The weight of the bobbin keeps the fly from unraveling. You can add weight to your bobbin by inserting lead into the spool before attaching it to the bobbin.

The most popular style of bobbin is the open-frame. Choose a bobbin that fits comfortably in the palm of your hand.

# Scissors

SCISSORS include: (1) surgical-style for delicate work; (2) serrated-blade for precision cutting; (3) ceramic-blade, which eliminates the need for sharpening; (4) fine-point and (5) curved-blade for close-in work; and (6) spring-type, excellent for palming.

The scissors you buy for fly tying should be very sharp and have a fine point for close-in work. Select models with stainless-steel or ceramic blades. Ceramics cost more but never need sharpening.

Many professional flytiers keep their scissors in the palm of their hand while they tie. It's a good habit to get into, and will save frustration and time otherwise spent looking for misplaced scissors. Spring-type scissors (left) are designed specifically for palming.

Sewing scissors work fine for flytiers with small hands, but most men find the finger holes too small.

# Hackle Pliers

# Hair Stackers

Hackle pliers simplify the job of winding hackle. Select a model that will grasp the hackle tip firmly without slipping. The jaws should not have any sharp edges that could cut the hackle.

If your hackle pliers are cutting too many hackle tips, dull the edges with a fine file or hook honer.

A hair stacker is an essential tool for aligning the tips of many types of fibers. To use a hair stacker, place the funnel into the stacker. Put a small clump of hair into the funnel, tips first, then tap the stacker firmly against a hard surface several times. Remove the funnel and grasp the tips of the hair fibers carefully. The tips should be perfectly aligned.

HACKLE-PLIER styles include: (1) duplex, with padded jaws; (2) traditional English; (3) teardrop, with fine-point jaws; (4) rotating, which reduce the chance of breaking hackle; and (5) rotating, with half-hitch tool at end of handle.

HAIR STACKERS include: (1) small stacker for small bundles of hair; (2) adjustable stacker for longer types of hair; and (3) magnum stacker for aligning larger bundles of hair when tying bass bugs.

OTHER TOOLS include: (1) whip-finish tool for tying a secure finishing knot at head of fly; (2) tweezers for holding small materials, and other tasks; (3) bodkin, or dubbing needle, for combing out underfur, applying head cement and many other tasks; (4) hair packer for building dense spun-deer-hair bodies; (5) small pliers with flat jaws for safely mashing down hook barbs, when desired; and (6) hackle gauge for sizing hackle feathers.

# Hooks

The hook is the foundation of any fly pattern. But the many different styles, shapes and sizes of hooks available can confuse the beginning flytier.

In most cases, however, the novice flytier need only be concerned with two hook styles: the dry-fly and wet-fly.

Hooks for dry flies are made with light-gauge wire to help them float on the surface. Wet-fly hooks, which include streamer and nymph hooks, are generally heavier, to help them sink quickly.

The size, length, wire and shape of a hook all determine how the finished pattern will look and behave on or in the water.

SIZE. The size of a hook is expressed by a number; the larger the number, the smaller the hook. For example, a #20 hook is smaller than a #10. Hooks larger than a size #1 are expressed as a number followed by a slash and a zero, such as "2/0." Hook sizes larger than 1/0 are in ascending numerical order; a size 5/0, for example, is larger than a 3/0.

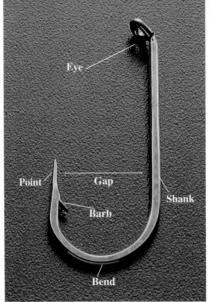

*Parts of a hook*

LENGTH. The length of a hook is expressed as standard, short or long. Any length other than standard is indicated by an "x." For example, a longer hook length may be described as "2x long"; shorter-than-standard, "2x short." The higher the x number, the longer or shorter the hook shank.

WIRE. The weight or gauge of the hook wire determines its suitability for a specific type of fly.

Hook weight other than standard is indicated by an "x." A slightly heavier-than-standard wire, for example, will be labeled as "1x heavy"; lighter, "1x light."

STYLES. Traditionally, hook style was indicated by names like "Limerick," "Sproat" and "Viking," which refer to the shape of the bend. Today, however, hook manufacturers are beginning to label hooks by function rather than style of bend. These include "caddis pupa," "streamer" and "flat-bodied nymph." Choose your hook depending on the type and size of fly you're tying.

HOOK EYES. Hooks come in three main eye types: turned-up eye (TUE), turned-down eye (TDE) or straight. Any one of these hooks will work for any fly; the choice depends on personal preference.

POPULAR HOOK SIZES for fly patterns range from size 18 to size 4. Larger hooks, from size 2 to 3/0, are used for specialty flies, including bass and salmon patterns. Hooks smaller than size 18 are used for tiny mayfly and midge imitations.

POPULAR HOOK STYLES include: (1) standard dry-fly, (2) swimming-nymph hook, (3) straight-eye; (4) flat-bodied nymph, (5) "Carrie Stevens" 10x long streamer; (6) caddis pupa; (7) 5X short with turned-up eye; (8) stinger nymph; and streamers with (9) turned-up and (10) turned-down eyes.

THREADS FOR FLY TYING include: (1) virtually un-breakable 1/0 Kevlar, (2) 3/0 Monocord, (3) fine-diameter 6/0 Fly Master, (4) extra-strong 3/0, (5) extra-fine 8/0. Apply additional wax to prewaxed thread (inset), if desired.

# Thread

Fly-tying thread secures the materials onto the hook while adding as little bulk as possible. When

*Antique 00, or 2/0, silk thread*

choosing fly-tying thread, consider diameter, material and strength.

Until recently, fly-tying thread was made of silk. And many flytiers still feel it is superior. But the majority of flytiers have turned to synthetic threads. Synthetics allow you to use finer-diameter threads without sacrificing strength; they come in a wider choice of colors, including fluores-cents; and, unlike silk, are available prewaxed, which means they hold materials better than silk does. Some flytiers add wax to prewaxed thread for greater adhesion.

Recent innovations in thread include new materials, such as Kevlar and Spectra, that are virtually un-breakable. These threads are used for tying large bass patterns. Another innovation is extra-fine-diameter thread, for tying very small flies.

Historically, thread size, or diameter, was indicated by a series of zeroes. The more zeroes, the smaller the diameter of the thread. These zeroes are now ab-breviated by a number followed by a zero; in other words, a 000 thread is labeled "3/0." A 3/0 thread has a larger diameter than a 6/0.

Common thread sizes range from 1/0, the largest, to 12/0, the smallest. Select the finest-diameter thread you can handle comfortably without breakage. Choose 3/0 to 12/0 for dry flies, wet flies and nymphs; 6/0 to 1/0 for streamers and bass patterns.

# Materials

The endless array of feathers, fur and man-made materials can be intimidating to the beginning flytier. Before you stock up, it's a good idea to study the recipes for the flies you plan to tie and familiarize yourself with the materials you'll need.

Fly-tying materials are divided into the following categories:

FEATHERS. The most commonly used feathers for fly tying are:

*Hackle feathers.* The term hackle has two different meanings in fly tying. It is used to describe the collar of fibers near the head of a fly; but it also refers to the neck, back or tail feathers of a domestic or wild fowl. These feathers are used for tying tails, wings and, of course, hackle.

When selecting hackle feathers, don't be confused by names like grizzly and badger. They're not types of material, just distinctive colors. Grizzly hackle, for instance, has well-defined black-and-white

HACKLE FEATHERS come from: (1) rooster saddle-hackle capes, (2) rooster neck-hackle capes and (3) hen neck-hackle cape. Individual feather types (inset) include: (4) rooster neck hackle, (5) spade hackle from rooster neck, (6) rooster saddle hackle, and (7) hen neck hackle.

HACKLE CAPES supply various-size feathers. (1) Large feathers can be found at the top of the cape; (2) smaller ones, at the bottom.

barring; badger is cream colored with a dark brown stripe along the stem.

Following are the three basic types of hackle feathers:

- Neck Hackle. Rooster neck hackle is long and narrow with straight, stiff fibers and a bright sheen. It is perfect for hackling dry flies. Hen neck hackle is more rounded at the tips and is commonly used for dry-fly wings. Neck hackle is usually sold as a complete skin, or *cape*, in a variety of natural and dyed colors.

- Saddle Hackle. The larger feathers from the back of a rooster or hen are called *saddle* hackle. These feathers have more soft, absorbant material, called *webbing*, close to the stem. Hen saddle hackle is commonly used for wet-fly collars.

- Spade Hackle. On a rooster cape, the large feathers at the sides are called *spade* hackle. Spade hackle fibers are used most often for dry-fly tails.

*Wing feathers.* Fibers from a primary wing feather of a turkey, duck or goose are commonly used for wings on wet and dry flies. Segments cut from a matching pair of primary feathers are used for making *quill-segment* wings (p. 62).

The short fibers on the leading edge of a duck, goose or turkey primary wing feather are called *biots*. They are commonly used for tailing nymph patterns (p. 41).

*Body, head and tail feathers.* Body feathers come from the flank, breast or back of any game bird or domestic fowl. They are used primarily for winging dry, wet and salmon flies. Crest feathers come from the top of the head; tippets, from the neck.

Tail feathers usually come from large, exotic birds, such as ostrich and peacock. The long, green

COMMON TYPES OF PRIMARY FEATHERS include: (1) duck, (2) goose, and (3) turkey. These feathers come in a wide range of natural and dyed colors.

BODY AND HEAD FEATHERS include: (1) turkey flat, (2) partridge, (3) grouse, (4) jungle cock, (5) Lady Amherst pheasant tippet, (6) guinea, (7) golden pheasant crest, (8) golden pheasant tippet, (9) silver pheasant, (10) mallard flank, (11) wood duck flank, (12) teal flank and (13) cul-de-canard (CDC), from oil-gland area of a duck.

23

OTHER FEATHER types include: (1) peacock sword; (2) eyed peacock tail, source of peacock herl; (3) pheasant tail; (4) ostrich tail, source of ostrich herl; and (5) turkey marabou feather.

COMMON HAIR types include: (1) natural and (2) bleached Texas whitetail body, (3) dyed and (4) natural northern whitetail body; (5) moose mane; (6) bleached elk body; (7) dyed bucktail; (8) squirrel tail; and (9) calf, or kip, tail.

strands of the peacock tail feather, called *herl*, are used for body material in countless fly patterns.

HAIR. One of the most versatile fly-tying materials is animal hair. The natural variations in color, size, density, buoyancy and texture make this material an essential part of any flytier's inventory.

Hair is used mainly for tails, wings and bodies on dry-fly patterns. It can also be used on bass bugs.

Common hair types include deer, elk, moose, calf and squirrel.

FUR. Finer in texture than hair, fur is used to make *dubbing*, which is applied to the tying thread. The dubbed thread is then wrapped around the shank of the hook to form a body (p. 48). The term dubbing also refers to this method of body construction.

Different fur colors, both dyed and natural, can be blended to form dubbed bodies that closely resemble those of real insects.

When blended with synthetic fibers, such as Antron or polypropylene, natural fur dubbing gains durability and sparkle.

Long, stiff fur fibers, called *guard* hairs, are used for making nymph bodies and the tails of some flies.

WOOL, FLOSS AND CHENILLE. Wool may be the oldest fly-tying material and is still an ingredient in many fly patterns. Wool remains popular for nymph and wet-fly bodies because it is highly absorbent.

Flosses and chenilles, originally made of silk, are now more commonly made from synthetics, such as rayon and nylon, and are available in a wider range of colors.

OTHER SYNTHETICS. Synthetic materials are used not only for making bodies, but also for creating realistic wings, legs, tails and ribbing. Synthetics are more durable than natural materials, and add sparkle, flash and fluorescence to some patterns.

POPULAR FUR TYPES and the dubbing they produce include: (1) Hare's mask, which has both short fur for dubbing and guard hairs for making tails; (2) otter; (3) muskrat; (4) black goat; (5) beaver; (6) red fox.

FLOSS, WOOL AND CHENILLE types include: synthetic floss in (1) two-strand, (2) four-strand and (3) single-strand; (4) wool yarn; synthetic chenille in (5) ultra-thin, (6) medium and (7) large diameter. See recipe catalogs for specific applications.

OTHER SYNTHETIC fly-tying materials include: (1) Flashabou, (2) Krystal Flash, (3) body foam, (4) Z-lon, (5) Rubber Legs, (6) polypropylene and (7) Antron yarns, (8) Swiss Straw, (9) Ultra Hair, (10) Mylar tinsel, (11) Lite-Brite, (12) Mylar body tubing, (13) V-rib and (14) Larva Lace ribbing. See recipe catalogs for specific applications.

ACCESSORIES to help organize your work space include: (1) incandescent, flexible-arm drafting lamp that can be clamped onto fly-tying bench; (2) multicompartment hardware cabinet with labeled drawers for organizing small tying tools and materials; (3) comfortable, height-adjustable secretary's chair that rolls, swivels and provides good back support; (4) 1-ft. by 2-ft. piece of green felt that can be spread out on fly-tying surface to prevent eyestrain and protect work surface from spills and scratches. Simply shake out felt and fold up for storage.

# Organizing Your
# Work Space

A well-organized work space can make your fly tying easier and more efficient.

Set up a fly-tying bench in a corner of the basement or spare bedroom, if possible. A comfortable chair will save your back, and a bright drafting lamp will reduce eyestrain.

For traveling, pack a few essential fly-tying tools and materials in a small tackle box (opposite), so you'll have everything you need to tie up a pattern to match the hatch.

KEEP your hook boxes in a well-labeled multicompartment storage box. It won't take up much space in your tying area, and you won't have to hunt for the right hooks.

DRILL different-size holes in a small block of wood or Styrofoam® to keep your fly-tying tools organized and close at hand.

KEEP a small box of moist towelettes on your tying bench. Some commercially dyed materials leave a stain on your fingers; wiping them with a moist towel will keep you from spreading the dye to other materials.

SIZE and sort your hackle feathers ahead of time. Store your presorted hackles in a labeled, sealable plastic bag for easy access when you need them.

USE an upside-down Post-It® note to hold your sized hackle feathers, quill segments or other tying materials. The tacky surface holds the feathers safely and gently until you are ready to use them.

CARRY a tackle box when you travel to hold your vise, tools and materials essential for tying flies on the spot.

Fly-Tying Basics

**DRY FLY**

Tail · Body · Wing · Head · Hackle

**NYMPH** — Ribbing · Abdomen · Wingcase · Thorax

**WET FLY** — Tag · Beard

**TERRESTRIAL** — Legs · Underbody

**STREAMER** — Butt

**BASS FLY** — Collar

BASIC PARTS OF A FLY, shown on the dry fly (top), include tail, body, wing, hackle and head. Other parts found on some, but not all, flies include ribbing, abdomen, wingcase and thorax, shown on the nymph; beard or throat, and tag, shown on the wet fly; legs and underbody, shown on the terrestrial; butt, shown on the streamer; and collar, shown on the bass fly.

# Steps to Tying a Fly

Once you are familiar with fly-tying tools and materials and you have a comfortable, well-lit work-space, you are ready to learn the basics of fly tying.

An artificial fly is made by winding one element after another — tail, body, wing, hackle and head — onto a hook. The secret to tying flies is understanding these elements and the techniques for combining them to create a complete fly.

This chapter is divided into eight sections (opposite), each covering a basic step in the fly-tying process. Often we'll show you different styles and techniques for completing each step.

## Basic Fly-tying Terms

Fly tying has a language of its own. In this book, most of the terms are defined or explained the first time they appear in the text. But here are a few terms to keep in mind when getting started:

*Tie-in point* — the place on the hook where the thread was started or the last material was tied to the shank.

*Forward* or *ahead* — toward the eye of the hook.

*Back* or *backward* — toward the rear or bend of the hook.

1 GETTING STARTED. This section shows you how to put a hook in the vise, start the thread on the hook and control thread and materials (pp. 32–35).

2 TAILS. The first ingredients in many fly patterns is the tail. In this section , you'll learn how to tie in several types of tails including hackle-fiber, hair, marabou and biot (pp. 36–41).

3 WEIGHTING THE HOOK. A good way to sink a nymph or streamer is to add weight to the hook before you tie in the body. This section shows you how to wrap lead wire around the shank or add a bead head to the hook (pp. 42–43).

4 RIBBING. This section shows you how to give any fly a segmented appearance by wrapping the body with materials such as floss, tinsel or wire (pp. 44–45).

5 BODIES. In this section you'll see how to tie bodies of dubbing, floss, herl, quill and deer hair (pp. 46–55).

6 WINGS. This section shows you how to tie a number of different wing types including upright-and-divided, caddis- or down-wing, tent-style and parachute-style (pp. 56–65).

7 HACKLE. Hackle can be used to imitate legs, fluttering wings or even gills. This section show you how to choose, prepare and wrap dry-fly, wet-fly, palmered and parachute-style hackle (pp. 66–71).

8 SALTWATER FLY-TYING BASICS. In this section you'll learn a number of techniques commonly used in tying saltwater fly patterns (pp. 72–79).

9 FINISHING KNOTS. When all the elements of a fly pattern have been wrapped onto the hook, it's important to finish your fly with a secure knot. You'll learn how to tie a half-hitch and use a whip-finish tool (pp. 80-81).

# Getting Started

The first step in tying a fly is setting the head of the vise at a 30- to 45-degree angle and placing the hook so the shank is horizontal.

The jaws of the vise should grasp the hook at the lower part of the bend (right), not at the point. Many beginning flytiers try to hide the hook point in the jaws to avoid catching a finger or cutting the thread. Not only does this increase the chance of thread tension breaking the hook, but the jaws cover the gap, which is used as a gauge for measuring some tying materials.

If you plan to mash down the barb of the hook, do it before you begin tying; if your hook breaks in the process, you won't lose a finished fly.

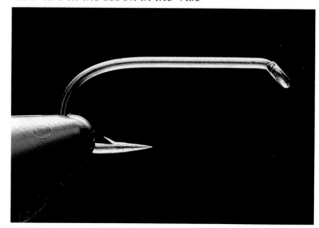

PLACE lower part of hook bend in jaws of vise, as shown. Tighten jaws just enough to hold hook securely without slippage; too much pressure can break hook. Spring-loaded vises adjust pressure automatically to hold most any size hook.

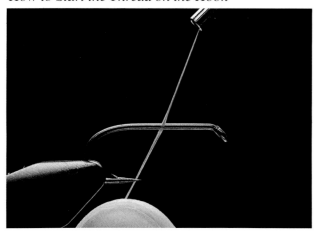

1 Place thread over hook at center of shank, as shown, with bobbin in your right hand and loose end of thread held firmly between left thumb and index finger.

2 Make several thread wraps forward toward eye of hook, keeping tension on the thread with both hands. Always wrap away from you over top of hook.

3 Wind thread back over first wraps. Practice keeping steady thread tension as you tie. Too much tension will break the thread, too little will allow materials to slip.

4 Trim off tag end of thread after it is secured by over-wraps. Keep tension on thread by letting bobbin hang below the hook.

5 For patterns that require tying in the tail first, continue wrapping thread back to about 1/16 inch from the start of the bend. Tie in the tail at this point. When wrapping near hook bend, angle thread away from hook point to avoid nicking or fraying the thread.

6 For patterns that require tying in the wings first, wrap thread forward again to about one-quarter hook-shank length from eye. Tie in the wings at this point.

# Controlling Thread and Materials

*The Soft-loop Method*

When materials are wrapped with thread, they tend to shift and spread around the shank of the hook. The problem is caused by the pressure of the thread against the materials.

One way to prevent this is to use the *soft-loop*, or *pinch*, method. Another is to use the *controlled-slide* method, which lets thread tension work for you. Both methods will save you time and frustration later on.

1 Hold materials between thumb and forefinger and position materials on hook shank. Raise bobbin above hook so thread is taut against near side of materials.

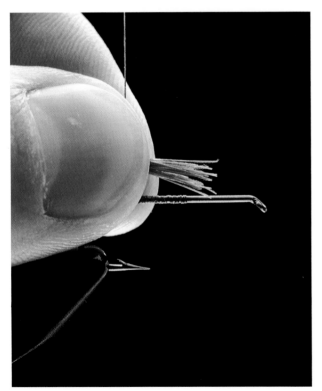

2 Pinch thread between thumb and forefinger to keep tension on thread and hold materials in place.

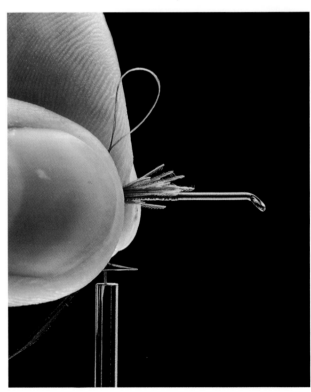

3 Form a slack, or soft, loop above materials. Bring thread back down other side of materials, and slide thread between thumb and forefinger without releasing the tension.

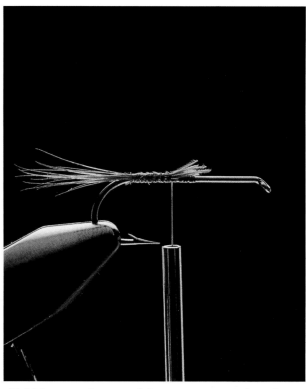

4 Slowly pull bobbin straight down, keeping pressure on thread and materials with thumb and forefinger.

5 Make several more soft loops to secure, and continue wrapping.

## The Controlled-slide Method

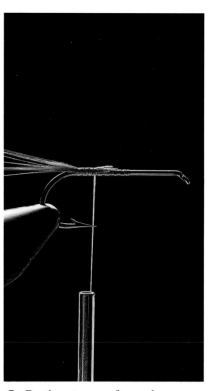

1 Position materials beside the hook shank at a slight angle as shown, to prevent them from spreading as you make first wrap.

2 Wrap thread over materials and around hook shank several times. Thread tension should slide materials onto top of hook.

3 Continue to wrap forward over materials to secure. Practice until you get a feel for the proper angle and thread tension.

# Tails

Most artificial flies just don't look right without a tail; after all, the majority of the naturals you're imitating have a tail of some type.

Whether it's the delicate hackle fibers of a tiny mayfly imitation, or the bushy clump of marabou on a large streamer, the tail of an artificial fly serves several purposes.

On a dry fly, for example, a few fibers tied in at the bend of the hook add realism and help support the fly on the surface of the water. On a subsurface pattern, downy feathers add a lifelike swimming action.

COMMON TAIL TYPES. Following are the four most widely used types of tails:

TAIL types include: (1) marabou, as shown on this Woolly Bugger streamer; (2) hackle-fiber, as on this Light Cahill dry fly; (3) biot, used to make the distinct forked tail on this Prince nymph; and (4) hair, shown on this Grizzly Wulff dry.

*Hackle-fiber.* Catskill flytiers of the early 1900s introduced dozens of delicate dry-fly patterns, with sparse tails made from the fine, straight fibers of a hackle feather.

Tails of this type are now the most common, not only on dry flies, but also on wet flies and nymphs. Hackle-fiber tails are made from rooster or hen hackle and resemble a natural insect tail. Other materials can be tied in as you would hackle fibers to create tails with a slightly different look.

Wood duck flank fibers, for instance, give the tail a barred effect. Lady Amherst pheasant tippet gives it a black-and-white coloration; golden pheasant, a striking gold-and-black.

Pheasant tail fibers, used mainly for nymphs, are thicker than hackle fibers, so they can be tied in to mimic individual tail filaments.

*Hair.* The late Lee Wulff popularized the use of animal hair, particularly deer and calf hair, in his very successful "Wulff"-style flies. These patterns are tied with bushy hair tails and wings, and were originally designed to withstand swift western rivers and huge Labrador brook trout.

Today, hair tails are used on many dry-fly patterns. Tails made from moose, calf and deer-body hair float well and are especially durable. Subsurface patterns often have tails made from rabbit-hide strips or squirrel tail to give them more action.

*Marabou.* Marabou tails seem to breathe and pulsate under water, giving almost any pattern a lifelike appearance. These downy feathers from the leg of a turkey are dyed in a wide range of colors, and are used for tailing streamers, nymphs and bass flies.

Pulsating tails can also be made from hen saddle-hackle feathers and the short strands of herl from a peacock sword feather (p. 24). These tails are tied in as you would marabou tails.

*Biot.* Tails made from biot fibers closely resemble the two splayed tail filaments of a natural stonefly nymph. But biots can also be used as a substitute for a hackle-fiber tail on many other nymphs and wet flies.

The pointed biot fibers come from the leading edge of a primary wing feather. The most popular sources are goose and duck, although pheasant and turkey biots also are used.

Many flies, particularly bass bugs and streamers, are tied with tails made from synthetic materials (p. 24), and you can substitute synthetics for natural materials in most patterns. Synthetics are generally more durable, flashy and colorful than natural fibers.

*Tips for Tying Tails*

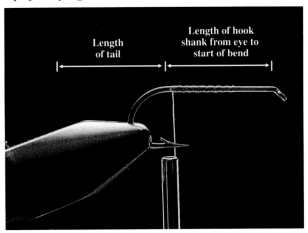

MEASURE tail fibers against hook shank. As a rule, length of tail on dry and wet flies should equal length of shank from hook eye to start of bend. Biot tails on nymphs are measured against hook gap (p. 41).

MAKE a tail that slants upward or a split tail by wrapping a small amount of dubbing (p. 47) onto hook shank at bend before tying in tail fibers.

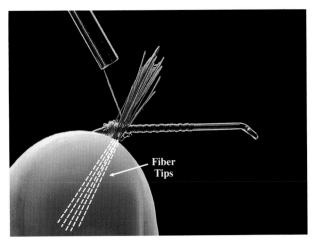

Fiber Tips

FAN tail fibers for more stability. Hold tips of fibers as shown (dotted line) and wrap with thread; fibers will spread horizontally, as on Grizzly Wulff (opposite).

## Hackle-fiber Tails

You can make hackle-fiber tails from any type of hackle. But spade-hackle fibers are best, because they are straight and stiff with very little webbing.

*Ginger-colored hackle fibers form the tail of this Ginger Fox dry fly*

*How to Tie In a Hackle-fiber Tail*

1 Select spade-hackle feathers from rooster neck cape in areas shown (dotted lines).

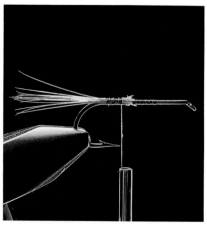

2 Pull a dozen or so fibers from stem. Grasp tips of fibers with your left hand and pull at 90-degree angle to keep tips aligned.

3 Size hackle fibers so they are slightly longer than hook shank. Tail should be same length as hook shank when tied in.

4 Position fibers on top of shank at hook bend. Tie in fibers with several soft loops.

5 Make several thread wraps to secure fibers. Wrap forward to middle of shank. Tail should now lie directly on top of shank.

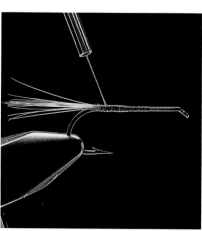

6 Wrap thread back to bend. You are now ready to tie in ribbing or body material.

# Hair Tails

Beginning flytiers should practice making hair tails using calf or elk hair; deer hair tends to flare around the hook shank. You'll need a hair stacker for aligning the tips.

*Calf hair is used to make the tail of this White Wulff dry fly*

## How to Tie In a Hair Tail

**1** Snip a small clump of calf, elk or deer hair fibers.

**2** Remove underfur by holding tips of fibers and combing a dubbing needle through butt ends.

**3** Place fibers into funnel of adjustable hair stacker, tips first. Tap stacker sharply on surface several times to align tips. Too much hair will prevent proper alignment.

**4** Remove funnel from stacker and carefully pull out fibers by the tips. Discard any short fibers.

**5** Measure fibers so tail will be same length as hook shank.

**6** Tie in fibers at bend, using several soft loops. Use moderate thread pressure near bend to minimize flaring; increase tension as you wrap forward. Trim excess butts.

## Marabou Tails

Marabou can be difficult to tie in because of the downy nature of the feather. But you can tame the fibers by stroking them with moistened fingers, as shown below.

*Marabou forms the tail of this Woolly Bugger*

### How to Tie In a Marabou Tail

1 Select a marabou feather. Separate tip fibers from lower fibers.

2 Stroke marabou tips with moistened fingers to keep downy fibers under control.

3 Measure marabou tip so tail will be same length as hook shank.

4 Tie in marabou feather on top of hook shank at bend, tips facing back, with several soft loops.

5 Wind thread forward over stem to secure. Trim off excess stem.

# Biot Tails

Biot tails are generally shorter than other types of tails and are tied in with a different technique. A mound of thread at the hook bend helps make the biots flare.

*Biot fibers form the tail and antennae of this Giant Black Stonefly Nymph*

## *How to Tie In a Biot Tail*

1 Snip two goose biots after bending stem. Set biots aside.

2 Start thread at midpoint of hook. Wind back to bend and form a small mound of thread.

3 Measure biot against hook; tail length should equal hook gap.

4 Place both biots in tail position, one on each side of hook, tips facing back. Secure butts with several soft loops just ahead of thread mound.

5 Wind thread back to middle of mound; this will make biot tips flare outward. Trim excess butts of biots.

# Weighting the Hook

Streamer and nymph patterns are often more effective when fished deep. Many fly anglers just pinch a split shot onto their leaders. But split shot can weaken a delicate leader, interfere with your casting or simply fall off.

The best way to get the fly down in the current is to add weight to the hook before tying the fly.

You can weight the hook by wrapping the shank with lead or a substitute, or adding a drilled metal bead as a head.

PATTERNS that can be tied with lead wire, or a substitute, include: (1) Pass Lake and (2) Peacock Caddis. Patterns with metal bead heads include: (3) Giant Black Stonefly, (4) Bottle Brush, (5) Thunderhead and (6) Pete's Pheasant Caddis.

MATERIALS for weighting hooks include: (1) light-gauge wire made from nontoxic lead substitute; (2) lead wire; (3) heavy-gauge lead-wire substitute; and metal beads in (4) brass, (5) copper, (6) nickel and (7) black finishes.

*How to Wrap a Hook with Lead*

1 Wind thread onto a nymph or streamer hook; wrap back to hook bend, and trim tag end.

2 Wrap a length of fine lead wire, or substitute, onto hook in middle of shank. Trim excess wire.

**3** Wind thread forward and back over wire in open spirals, leaving a little space between each turn. Make several thread turns in front of wire to secure.

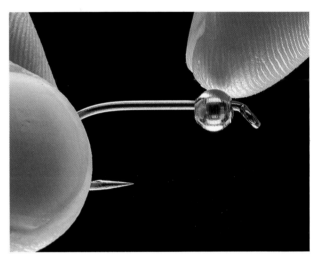

**4** Continue wrapping until wire is just covered with layer of thread. Apply a coat of head cement, if desired. Continue tying pattern.

## How to Add a Bead Head

**1** Place nymph or streamer hook in vise. Mash down barb with small pliers to allow bead to slide over barb.

**2** Remove hook from vise, and slide bead onto shank. Bead should rest against hook eye.

**3** Replace hook in vise, wrap thread onto hook at midpoint of shank and trim tag end.

**4** Wind thread forward and build a small mound of thread to hold bead in place. Continue tying pattern.

*Tinsel ribbing adds flash, durability and a realistic, segmented appearance to this (1) Llama streamer, (2) March Brown dry fly and (3) Gold-ribbed Hare's Ear soft-hackle fly.*

# Ribbing

Many aquatic insects have segmented bodies. A few wraps of ribbing give the body a segmented look while adding durability and flash to most any fly pattern.

Experiment with various styles and colors of ribbing, even if the fly recipe doesn't call for it.

Flies with bodies made of biot or stripped quill (p. 52) appear segmented without additional ribbing material.

RIBBING MATERIALS include: (1) thread, (2) floss, (3) fine gold oval tinsel, (4) medium silver oval tinsel, (5) Mylar flat tinsel, (6) V-rib, (7) Larva Lace and (8) stripped grouse tail. Small motors (inset) are a good source for copper-wire ribbing.

1 Cut a 3-inch length of ribbing material; allow enough material for tying in, wrapping and tying off. Ribbing material should be tied in *before* adding body material.

2 Tie in ribbing material on top of hook shank. Leave a tag end about ½ inch long. Make several thread wraps to secure.

3 Loop tag end of ribbing material back over itself, and secure with several turns of thread. Trim tag.

4 Add body material, such as chenille.

5 Wind ribbing forward over body material with four to six evenly spaced open-spiral wraps.

6 Secure ribbing with several turns of thread; trim excess ribbing material. Continue tying pattern.

# Bodies

Most flies have a simple body made of one or two elements; others, including many streamers, nymphs and wet flies, have very complex bodies.

BODY ELEMENTS. Following are the most common body elements, and definitions of each:

*Wingcase* — The protrusions on top of many nymph patterns, representing undeveloped wings.

*Abdomen* — The long, usually thin, part of the fly that begins just behind the wings or wingcase.

*Thorax* — The shorter, thicker section near the front of the fly.

*Tag* — A few turns of contrasting-color thread, floss or tinsel at or near the hook bend.

*Butt* — Several turns of material, such as herl, at the bend of hook; usually thicker than the tag.

*Head* —Made with extra thread wraps, by leaving butt ends of wing fibers exposed and trimming them, or by clipping spun deer hair to the desired shape.

*Eyes* — Sometimes added to patterns for more realism. The most common types are:

- Doll eyes. Available at most fly and hobby shops, these eyes are attached to the finished fly with waterproof glue.

- Painted. You can form eyes with dabs of acrylic paint (p. 77).

- Monofilament. Tie in a short length of heavy mono across the hook shank and lightly burn the ends to form eyes.

- Bead-chain. A length of standard bead chain will make several pairs of eyes. Snip a two-bead section and tie it in across the shank.

BODY styles include: (1) floss, in Tellico nymph; (2) spun deer hair, in Goddard Caddis dry fly; (3) quill, in Borcher Special dry; (4) dubbed, in Light Cahill dry and (5) Gold-bead Possie nymph; (6) herl, in Peacock Caddis dry.

- Hourglass. Available in many sizes and colors, these eyes are attached by tying the neck across the shank.

BODY STYLES. Body styles of artificial flies range from the highly realistic to the fanciful. How a fly looks on or in the water depends on the materials and techniques you use to create the body. The five basic fly body styles include:

*Dubbed.* The most common type of body material, dubbing can be used to produce a variety of body shapes and thicknesses for almost all types of flies. Materials for dubbed bodies range from beaver and rabbit to synthetics, such as Antron.

*Floss, wool and chenille.* Available in both silks and synthetics, floss is used to form a fine, smooth body profile. It is also used to form a base layer, or *underbody,* that is wrapped with body material of contrasting color or texture.

Wool yarn, a traditional body material, forms a slightly thicker profile than floss.

Chenille is a yarnlike material, either silk or synthetic, which has a fuzzy texture that gives subsurface flies a pulsating action. Thin chenille is popular for small nymph bodies; thicker chenille, for bulky nymphs, streamers and bass bugs.

*Herl.* Herl is used mainly for dry flies, wet flies and nymphs, but many fly fishermen believe that it increases the effectiveness of any fly. This material, most commonly from the large tailfeather of a peacock, has a natural sheen that appeals to trout. Like wool yarn and chenille, herl is wrapped around the shank of the hook to form a bulky body.

You can form a thinner herl-style body by wrapping the hook with fibers from the tail or wing of other birds, such as pheasant or duck.

*Quill.* Although the term "quill" commonly refers to the stem of a large feather, in fly tying, it describes a fly body style. Quill bodies simulate the shiny, segmented look of a natural mayfly and are used on many dry- and wet-fly patterns.

The traditional source of quill is peacock herl with the fibers removed to expose the stem. Stripped hackle stems, biot fibers and grouse tail are substitutes for herl. Moose mane has black-and-white fibers that also make an excellent quill-like body.

*Spun deer hair.* The hollow fibers of deer-body hair make it unbeatable for tying bass bugs. The technique of allowing deer-hair fibers to flare around the shank of the hook is called *spinning.* Spun deer hair floats well and can be lightly trimmed to create a fat mouse- or froglike appearance for bass and pike patterns, or tightly clipped to form a dry-fly body.

*Tips for Making Bodies*

TAPER dubbed mayfly bodies slightly thicker at center of shank than at tail to mimic the natural.

TAPER dubbed caddis bodies slightly thicker at tail than at head so wing lies flush over body.

CHOOSE a thread color that matches the color of the body material to make the thread less visible.

*This Damselfly nymph has a heavily dubbed body*

## Dubbed Bodies

As a rule, the dubbing on dry-fly bodies is thinner than that on wet flies or nymphs. This way, dry flies are light enough to float high, and their slim profile looks like that of an adult aquatic insect. To accomplish this, use a fine fur dubbing material, such as beaver, rabbit or muskrat.

Nymphs are usually dubbed to look fatter by adding more dubbing material to the thread and using thicker fur, such as fox, goat or the guard hair of hare's mask.

Synthetic fibers, or a combination of natural and synthetic, are also used for dubbing. Synthetics, however, can be tricky for the beginning flytier to control, because the fibers are longer and stretchier than fur.

You can add ribbing material to dubbed bodies to give the fly a segmented look.

### How to Dub a Dry Fly, Mayfly Style

1 Apply a small amount of fly-tying wax to thread, if desired. Although most fly-tying thread is prewaxed, adding more wax to thread or to your fingers will help you form a tightly dubbed body.

2 Remove a small pinch of dubbing material, about the size of a dime, from package.

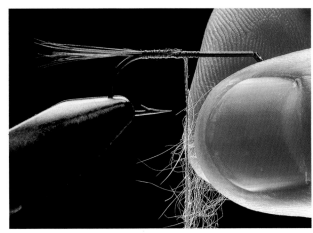

3 Separate fibers of dubbing material to eliminate any clumps.

4 Apply a few fibers at a time to thread. Spin fibers firmly onto thread between your thumb and forefinger. Spin fibers in one direction only, or you will rub them off with every other spin.

5 Apply dubbing to three inches of thread. First inch should be only slightly thicker than thread itself. Add more dubbing below first inch until you see a slight increase in thread thickness.

6 Wrap dubbed thread back to hook bend, then reverse direction and wrap forward.

7 Continue wrapping dubbed thread forward around hook shank. The slightly thicker dubbing on last two inches of thread forms a tapered body.

8 Wind dubbed thread forward to about midpoint of shank. Pull any remaining dubbing from the thread so you can continue to wind on materials.

*Yellow floss forms the body of this Caterpillar terrestrial pattern*

## Floss, Wool and Chenille Bodies

Most floss bodies are tied with multistrand material, but for small or delicate flies, all you need is a single strand of floss.

Wool and chenille bodies are tied in much the same way as the floss body below.

### How to Form a Floss Body

1 Cut an 8-inch length of multistrand floss.

2 Tie in strands of floss at hook bend with several turns of thread. Wind thread forward over tag ends of floss to ⅛ inch behind eye.

3 Grasp ends of strands; wrap floss forward around shank.

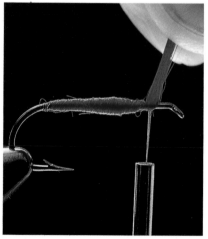

4 Form tapered body by slightly overlapping previous wraps as you wind forward.

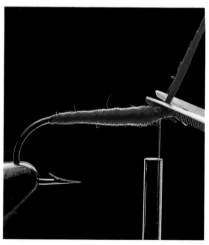

5 Secure strands with several thread turns; trim excess floss.

## Herl Bodies

Herl is commonly used as the main body material, but it also makes a good underbody, butt or palmered-style (p. 70) body wrapping.

Because herl is one of the most fragile body materials, many flytiers add ribbing for durability.

*Peacock herl is used to tie this Theo's Danger Baby nymph*

### How to Tie a Herl Body

1 Snip two or three strands of herl from a large peacock tail feather.

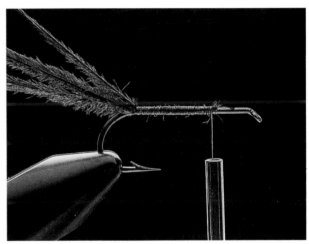

2 Tie in strands near hook bend with tips facing back. Secure strands with several turns of thread. Wrap thread forward over butt ends to a point one-third hook-shank length behind eye.

3 Grasp the tip of one strand of herl with hackle pliers. Wrap herl forward around hook shank, and secure.

4 Grasp second strand with hackle pliers, wind forward and secure.

5 Wind third strand forward and secure. Trim ends of all strands and continue adding materials.

*This classic Quill Gordon has a body of stripped peacock herl*

# Quill Bodies

One of the best materials for making quill bodies is herl from the tip of an eyed peacock feather. Herl strands from this part of the feather have stems with distinct light and dark edges, which give the body a striped appearance. Carefully strip the fibers from the stem using your fingers or a pencil eraser (below).

For a raised ribbing effect, make a quill body using biots (opposite).

## How to Make a Quill Body from Stripped Peacock Herl

1 Pull a strand of peacock herl from an eyed peacock tail feather.

2 Place strand of herl on tying surface and carefully rub off fibers with eraser. Too much pressure may break the fragile stem.

3 Moisten stripped stem with water to reduce brittleness and prevent it from splitting as you wrap.

4 Tie in stem about one-third hook-shank length from bend. Wrap thread forward.

5 Wind stem back toward bend in an open spiral.

6 Reverse direction, and wrap stem forward in a tight spiral. Each wrap should touch previous wrap, to form smooth body profile.

7 Secure stem with several turns of thread. Trim excess stem.

8 Apply thin coating of lacquer to quill body for durability.

## How to Make a Quill Body from Biot

1 Snip one biot from stem with scissors.

2 Tie in tip of biot at hook bend with several turns of thread. Wind thread forward as shown.

3 Grasp butt end of biot with hackle pliers and wrap forward around hook shank.

4 Secure biot with several turns of thread, and trim excess biot. Apply lacquer, if desired.

*Several colors of dyed deer hair give this Deer-hair Bug its unique appearance*

## Spun Deer-hair Bodies

Spinning deer hair isn't difficult, but it takes some practice to learn and it's messy! Allow yourself plenty of time for mistakes and don't try it in the living room.

The trick to spinning deer hair is to use as much thread tension as possible without breaking the thread or bending the hook. Use a strong thread, such as Monocord or Kevlar. You'll want to use a hair packer (p. 19) to ensure a compact body.

Bass flies are tied with many deer-hair bundles, which are lightly trimmed to form bulky bodies. Dry flies require only a few small bundles, trimmed closely.

Deer hair comes dyed in practically every color. To create a multicolored body, alternate the color of the hair bundles you tie in along the shank.

### *How to Make a Spun Deer-hair Body*

1 Clip a small bundle of deer hair from hide. Do not use too much hair at one time; the body of a bass bug is built of many small clumps tied in and packed.

2 Comb out the underfur with a dubbing needle, making sure all the downy fibers have been removed.

3 Snip off tips of deer hair, which are too fine to flare.

4 Hold deer hair by tips, and position bundle over hook shank at bend. Make several soft loops around middle of bundle to secure on top of shank.

5 Apply downward pressure on thread. Both ends of deer hair will begin to flare. Make several more thread turns through hair, keeping firm tension on thread.

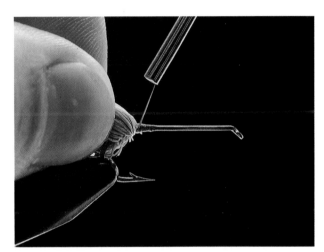

6 Draw fibers back with fingers, and make several thread wraps around shank in front of deer hair.

7 Push hair back toward bend with hair packer. This will make the body denser and easier to trim to the proper shape.

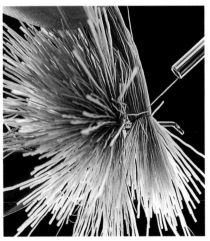

8 Add another small bundle of deer hair, repeating steps 3 through 7 until shank is filled. Leave room at hook eye, and whip-finish (p. 73).

9 Trim body to appropriate shape with scissors or razor blade.

WING styles and materials include: upright-and-divided, tied with (1) hair on White Wulff, (2) duck flank on Dark Hendrickson, (3) quill segment on Black Gnat, (4) hackle tips on Adams; caddis, tied with (5) hair on Elk Hair Caddis; down-wing, tied with (6) quill segment on March Brown; and parachute, tied with (7) hair on Light Cahill.

# Wings

Wings imitate the profile of a natural insect. On dry flies, they also add visibility so the angler can better see the fly on the water, and they slow the fly's descent so it settles gently to the surface. On wet flies and streamer patterns, they add color or action.

A few strands of material of contrasting color are sometimes added to the top of the wing of a streamer or wet fly to form an *overwing* or *topping*, or beneath the wing to form an *underwing*. Contrasting materials tied to each side of the wing are simply called *sides*.

*Cheeks*, usually eyed jungle cock feathers, are also tied to the side of the wing of many wet-fly and streamer patterns.

When tying wings on any pattern, proportion is important (opposite). Wings that are too large can affect the balance of the fly, causing it to float on its side. Undersize wings will not produce the proper silhouette.

BASIC WING STYLES. Most fly wings fall into one of the following categories:

WRAP hook shank with thread to form a base for tying in the wings.

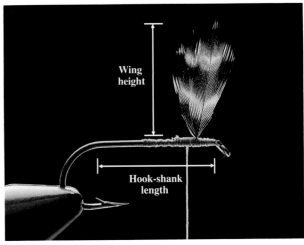

PROPORTION upright wing so it is equal in height to hook-shank length when tied in.

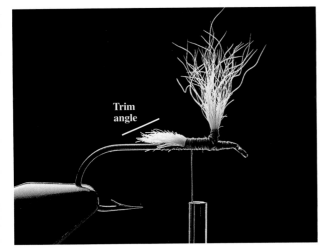

TRIM butt ends of wing material at an angle before over-wrapping with thread, for a tapered body.

CLIP a duck wing-quill segment 1 1/2 times wider than the desired finished wing size. Segment will compress when tied in.

*Upright-and-divided.* Intended to imitate the wings of a natural mayfly or midge, upright-and-divided wings are the most common dry-fly wing style. The wings are tied in so they project at about a 45-degree angle from either side of vertical.

In a *spent-wing* pattern, a variation of the upright-and-divided style, the wings are tied to project at a 90-degree angle. This way, the wings rest on the surface, like the wings of a spent mayfly.

Spent wings are tied in just like upright-and-divided wings; simply cinch them down to the sides more to make them spread.

*Caddis, Down-wing and Tent.* These wing styles are tied in to lie flat or angle back over the body of the fly. They are used on wet flies, streamers and dry flies, particularly caddisfly and stonefly imitations.

Caddis and down-wing styles are similar, but caddis wings are shorter, resembling the mothlike wing of a caddisfly.

Tent-style wings are made with a folded quill segment, tied in over the back to mimic the folded wings of an adult insect.

*Parachute.* Used only on surface patterns, the parachute-style wing forms the base around which the hackle is wrapped horizontally. This wing-and-hackle combination causes the fly to settle slowly to the water, like a parachute, and ride low in the surface film.

These basic wing types can be tied with a variety of materials, each requiring a slightly different tying technique. Refer to pages 58 to 65 for instructions on tying the most popular wing styles.

*A Hendrickson is tied with duck-flank wings, upright-and-divided*

# Duck-flank Wings, Upright-and-divided

The barring on these delicate feathers makes them the best imitation of a natural mayfly wing. When tied in, the wing has a natural mottled look and gives the illusion of fluttering.

Wood duck flank feathers are preferred for these wings, because of their distinct barring. But you can substitute teal or dyed mallard-flank feathers.

## *How to Tie In Duck-flank Wings, Upright-and-divided*

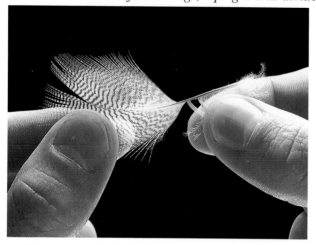

1 Select a large flank feather with a naturally squared-off end. Prepare feather by stripping away soft, downy fibers near base.

2 Fold feather lengthwise down the stem, with shiny side out.

3 Measure folded feather so height of finished wing equals hook-shank length.

4 Position wing material over tie-in point, just ahead of midpoint of shank, tips facing forward. Tie in feathers, using several soft loops. Leave room between wing and hook eye for tying in hackle.

5 Wrap thread back toward bend to secure fibers. Trim off excess stem. Wind thread forward to tie-in point.

6 Set wings upright by grasping tips between thumb and forefinger. Make several turns of thread around hook shank in front of wings.

7 Divide fibers into two equal parts with dubbing needle or tips of scissors. Separate wings by gently pulling them to the sides.

8 Pass thread between wings from front to back, crossing over shank.

9 Bring thread around underside of hook and pass forward between wings, in a figure-eight pattern. Make a second figure eight.

10 Make one complete thread turn around base of far wing. Pass bobbin under shank, then make one complete turn around near wing.

11 Make several turns of thread around hook shank to secure wings. Wind thread back to hook bend, then add remaining materials.

## Hair Wings, Upright-and-divided

*This durable Royal Humpy has upright-and-divided hair wings*

Hair wings are set upright-and-divided in much the same way as duck-flank wings. Usually made of deer, calf or elk hair, or a synthetic substitute, these wings are durable, buoyant and are easy for the fisherman to see on the surface of the water.

*How to Tie In Hair Wings, Upright-and-divided*

1 Snip a small bundle of hair from the hide. Comb out any underfur with a dubbing needle. Place hair in funnel of hair stacker, tips first.

2 Tap stacker sharply against surface to align tips. Remove funnel from stacker, and pull fibers from bottom of funnel carefully by the tips.

3 Transfer butts to left hand, and measure fibers to proper length. Hair wings should be equal in height to shank length.

4 Tie in hair bundle, tips facing forward, on top of shank with several soft loops.

5 Trim off butt ends at an angle; wrap thread back over tapered cut to form a smooth foundation for the body material.

6 Set wings upright and divide as shown in steps 6 through 11 of duck-flank wings (p. 59).

# Hair Wings, Caddis- and Down-wing Style

In caddis patterns, the mothlike wings are slightly shorter than the hook shank, when tied in. In down-wing patterns, the wings are equal to, or slightly longer than, the hook shank.

*The wings on this Elk-hair Caddis are tied in over the body*

*How to Tie In Hair Wings, Caddis-style*

1 Tie in body material. Leave about one hook-eye length gap behind eye; wrap the gap with thread to form base for wing.

2 Hold a small bundle of stacked hair by the butts; it should equal hook shank in length. Turn hair bundle around, and position over hook shank with tips facing toward hook bend.

3 Make one complete turn of thread around bundle of elk hair only, then make another around bundle and hook shank.

4 Cinch bundle on top of shank, and make several wraps to secure. Hair should not spin around shank. Whip-finish, and trim off thread.

5 Trim butt ends of elk hair at a slight angle to form a small, tapered head. Apply head cement to thread wraps for added durability.

## Quill-segment Wings, Upright-and-divided

*The Black Gnat is tied with quill-segment wings, upright-and-divided*

For upright-and-divided wings, select a pair of matched quill feathers from opposite wings and tie them in before adding body material.

Quill segments may separate when you tie them in, but if you stroke the segments, the tiny barbules will lock the fibers together. Adding a drop of head cement to each segment before tying it in will reduce the chance of splitting.

### *How to Tie In Quill-segment Wings, Upright-and-divided*

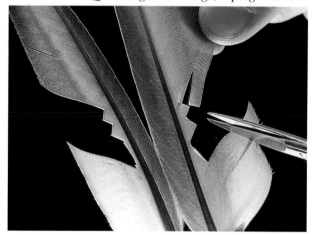

1 Select a matched pair of quill feathers from opposite wings. Snip a ¼-inch segment from the same place on each feather.

2 Place segments back-to-back, with shiny sides together and tips aligned, so they flare slightly. Measure segments to same length as hook shank.

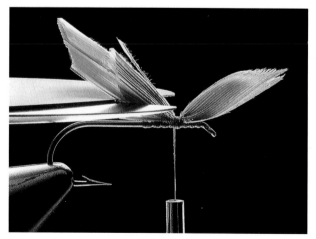

3 Position segments over hook shank, curved side up, with tips facing forward. Tie in, using several soft loops. Trim butts, and secure ends with thread wraps.

4 Set wings upright with several turns of thread around hook shank in front of wings.

## Quill-segment Wings, Tent-style

For tent-style wings, tie in the body material first. Then select a single quill segment, fold it as shown below and tie it in.

You can also tie a two-segment, tent-style wing as on the Henryville Caddis (right). Simply tie in one folded segment on top of another segment of approximately the same size.

*The Henryville Caddis is tied tent-style, using two quill segments*

### How to Tie In Quill-segment Wings, Tent-style

1 Snip one ¼-inch-wide segment from the wing quill feather. For a two-segment wing, select a matched pair of quills.

2 Position quill segment(s) over hook shank, tip facing back. Tie in with several soft loops, and trim butt end.

3 Gently fold quill segment(s) lengthwise along center to form tent shape.

4 Cut tip of segment(s) to proper length, which is slightly longer than the hook itself. Cut each side at an angle to form a "V," if desired.

# Hackle-point Wings, Upright-and-divided

Hackle-point wings are made from the tips, or points, of a hackle feather. They produce a realistic wing profile, but add very little weight to the finished fly.

Traditional hackle-point wings were made from rooster hackle. But the tips of modern rooster hackle are too narrow for the proper wing profile. As a result, flytiers now use the tips of hen neck hackle feathers, which are broader and more rounded.

*This Mosquito pattern is tied with grizzly hackle-point wings*

## *How to Tie In Hackle-point Wings*

1 Select two medium-size hackle feathers. Align back-to-back so tips flare slightly.

2 Measure hackles; finished wing should equal hook shank in length. Trim hackle fibers from stem, leaving just the tips, or points, to form wings.

3 Position hackle points over hook shank, tips facing forward, and tie in with several soft loops.

4 Trim off stems, and set wings upright-and-divided (p. 59). Wrap thread back to hook bend, and continue tying pattern.

# Parachute-style Wings

A parachute wing gives a dry fly a unique profile easily seen by fish and angler. The wing also serves as a base for wrapping the parachute-style, or horizontal, hackle (p. 71). This type of hackle causes the fly to float low in the surface film, much like an emerging mayfly.

Parachute wings can be made from many materials, including duck-flank fibers, hackle tips, calf tail and a variety of synthetic fibers. Use bright white or orange poly-yarn wing materials for extra visibility in low-light situations.

*Parachute-style wing and hackle are seen in this Pink Lady pattern*

## How to Tie In a Parachute-style Wing

1 Select a small bundle of calf tail hair. Measure material so wing height equals hook-shank length.

2 Tie in bundle with tips facing forward, as you would an upright-and-divided wing. Trim butt ends and wrap thread over them to form tapered base for body.

3 Set wing upright with several turns of thread around hook shank in front of wing.

4 Wrap thread horizontally around upright wing to form a 1/8-inch-high base for hackle. Add hackle as shown on page 71.

# Hackle

Hackle gives an artificial fly the illusion of life. It is used on most patterns to imitate legs, fluttering wings or pulsating gills.

Types of hackle include:

*Dry-fly hackle* — Made from the stiff, straight neck feathers of a rooster, this hackle forms the collar that gives a dry fly its characteristic profile and keeps it riding high on the water.

*Wet-fly hackle* — Used on both wet and soft-hackle flies, this type of hackle is made from hen-neck, saddle-hackle or partridge feathers, which are softer and more absorbant than dry-fly hackle.

Wet-fly hackle is first folded (right), so all the fibers are on one side of the stem and slant back over the body of the fly when tied in.

Wet-fly hackle is sometimes modified to form a *beard*, or *throat*, on the underside of the fly. With the top fibers trimmed away, the remaining fibers imitate the folded legs of an insect. You can also make a beard by tying fibers to the bottom of the hook shank.

*Palmered hackle* — Palmered hackle adds bulk without adding weight. Palmered rooster hackle makes dry flies float higher; hen hackle gives nymphs and wet flies lively action under water.

*Parachute hackle* — Parachute-style flies float lower in the water than standard dries. They rest in, not on, the surface, resembling natural emergers.

The effectiveness of parachute patterns leads many flytiers to experiment with this hackle on traditional fly patterns.

Choose stiff, straight rooster-neck hackle feathers, as you would for hackling dry flies.

HACKLE styles include: (1) palmered, as on this Wooly Worm wet fly; (2) parachute, as on this Light Cahill Parachute; (3) wet-fly, as on this Gold-ribbed Hare's Ear soft-hackle; and (4) dry-fly, as on this Brown Bivisible.

## How to Measure Hackle

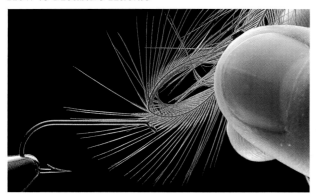

HOOK-LENGTH METHOD. Measure hackle against hook shank by bending feather as shown. As a rule, dry-fly, palmered and parachute-style hackle should be three-fourths hook-shank length, when tied in. Wet-fly hackle should equal length of shank. *Note:* never trim tips of hackle to achieve desired length.

HACKLE-GAUGE METHOD. Use a hackle gauge to select the correct-size feather. Bend feather around post so tips cover lines on gauge. For dry-fly, palmered and parachute-style hackle, match fiber length to the size hook you are using, as indicated by numbers on gauge. Wet-fly hackle should be slightly longer for a given hook size.

## How to Prepare Hackle

TRIM off soft, downy fibers, or webbing, near base of feather, leaving fiber stubs to help thread secure hackle. Snip off butt end, leaving approximately ¼ inch of trimmed portion.

## How to Use Hackle Pliers

GRASP tip of feather with hackle pliers so stem and pliers are aligned. If you grasp feather crosswise, you are more likely to break off tip. Wind at a right angle to shank, using only enough pressure to keep hackle in place; too much will break tip of feather.

## How to Fold Wet-fly Hackle

1 Select one large saddle-hackle, hen-neck hackle or partridge feather. Stroke all fibers back toward base of feather so they are at a right angle to stem.

2 Grasp tip of feather, shiny side up, in right hand; hold base of feather in left hand as shown.

3 Stroke fibers downward between left thumb and forefinger until all fibers are folded to one side of stem.

## Dry-fly Hackle

Dry-fly hackle is wound around the hook shank at wing position. The fibers radiate at a right angle to the shank to form the familiar collar.

On most dry flies, the hackle is about three-fourths the length of the hook shank.

*Straight, stiff hackle fibers make up the hackle and body of this Brown Bivisible dry fly*

### *How to Tie In Dry-fly Hackle*

1 Select two rooster-neck hackle feathers of the proper size, and trim webbed portion. Align tips of feathers with shiny sides toward you. Place them alongside shank at base of wings, tips facing backward at a 30-degree angle.

2 Secure hackle stems with two turns of thread behind wing, then two in front. Trim any excess hackle stems.

3 Using hackle pliers, grasp the tip of the hackle farthest away from you. Pull hackle straight down below hook to begin winding.

4 Make several turns behind wing, then several in front. Wrap over hackle tip with thread to secure. Trim off hackle tip.

5 Grasp second hackle tip and weave it through first with a zig-zag motion to avoid crushing fibers of first hackle. Wrap thread over second tip to secure; trim tip.

# Wet-fly Hackle

Wet-fly hackle must be folded before it is tied in (p. 67). This way the fibers angle backward, giving the fly a streamlined shape.

Wet-fly hackle should be slightly longer than dry-fly hackle, or about hook-shank length when tied in.

*Black hen hackle fibers slope back over the body of this Hen-and-Brown soft-hackle fly*

## How to Tie In Wet-fly Hackle

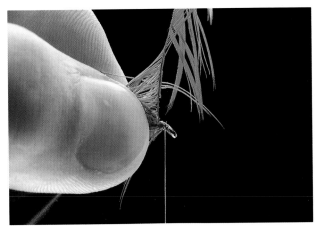

1 Select and measure one large saddle hackle feather. Do not trim webbing; it absorbs water and helps sink the fly.

2 Fold hackle feather; then tie in tip just in front of body material. Make several turns of thread to secure. Trim off excess hackle tip.

3 Wrap hackle once around shank of hook, then stroke fibers back with fingers.

4 Make two more wraps, stroking fibers back after each wrap. Make several turns of thread to secure. Trim excess hackle stem.

## Palmered Hackle

Palmered hackle is wrapped in an open spiral over body materials, such as floss, chenille or dubbing. It should be the same length as dry-fly hackle, or slightly shorter.

Some flytiers wrap fine copper-wire ribbing over palmered hackle for added strength and durability.

*Grizzly hackle is palmered over peacock herl on this Griffith's Gnat*

### How to Tie In Palmered Hackle

1 Select a dry-fly hackle feather of the proper size. Trim webbed portion.

2 Place butt of hackle alongside hook shank at bend, with tip facing back. Secure with several turns of thread. Trim excess butt.

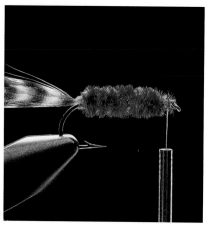

3 Tie in body material, wrap forward and secure.

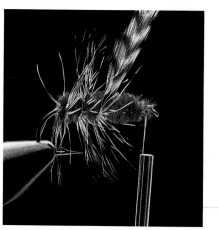

4 Wind hackle forward over body in evenly spaced open spirals, using hackle pliers.

5 Secure hackle tip with thread; trim excess tip.

# Parachute Hackle

Parachute hackle is wrapped horizontally around an upright wing of natural or synthetic fibers.

Although parachute hackle is the same length as dry-fly hackle, it is tied with only one hackle feather, instead of two.

*Parachute hackle is wound horizontally around the base of the wing on this Light Cahill*

## *How to Tie In Parachute Hackle*

1 Tie in an upright, parachute-style wing (p. 65). Select a dry-fly hackle feather of proper size, and trim webbed portion.

2 Position hackle feather alongside hook shank at base of wing. Tie in hackle feather, shiny side up, with tip pointing back.

3 Grasp tip with hackle pliers and wrap hackle three times around base of wing to form horizontal collar.

4 Pull hackle fibers back gently with fingers, so you can tie off without wrapping over hackle. Make several thread turns around stem and shank to secure. Trim excess hackle tip.

# Saltwater Fly-Tying Basics

Most saltwater fly patterns call for the same basic tying techniques presented in the previous pages. But following are a number of techniques and elements commonly used in tying saltwater flies. These techniques include:

EYES. Already described on page 46, eyes are a particularly important ingredient in saltwater patterns. In this section you'll learn how to tie in bead-chain,

dumbbell, plastic molded, doll-type, hairbrush, burned mono, adhesive, and painted eyes.

BODIES. In addition to the traditional bodies described on pages 46 through 55, several styles of bodies are essential to tying saltwater patterns. These include: Braided-tube bodies, epoxy bodies, crab bodies, and tarpon-fly style bodies.

## Types of Saltwater Hooks

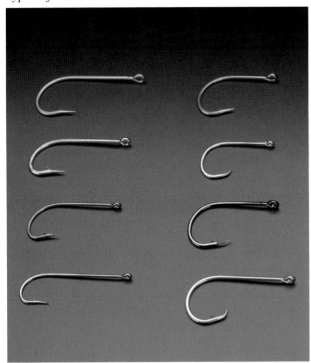

POPULAR HOOKS for saltwater flies include: (top to bottom, left) TMC 811S, Gamakatsu SL11-3H, Mustad 34007, Mustad 34011; (top to bottom, right) Mustad C68S SS, Gamakatsu SC16, TMC 600SP, and Mustad C71S SS.

## Types of Epoxies and Adhesives

EPOXIES AND ADHESIVES for saltwater flies include: five-minute type epoxy, hot-melt glue sticks and gun, Super Glue, Goop, and UV Knot Sense with UV light.

## Types of Thread

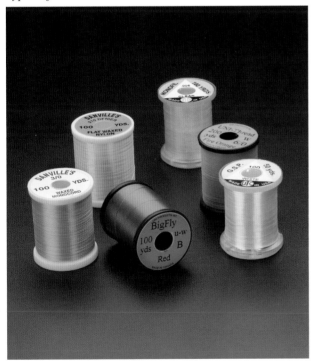

POPULAR THREAD TYPES include: Danville 3/0 Monocord, flat waxed nylon, UNI BigFly, monofilament thread, Uni-Thread 6/0, and GSP 100.

## Types of Markers and Paints

POPULAR MARKERS AND PAINTS for saltwater flies include: model paint, Sharpies, and Prismacolor markers.

*The eyes on this Bigeye Tarpon fly are painted.*

## Eyes

Many saltwater anglers believe that predator gamefish will follow and strike at the eyes of a baitfish. Eyes can make a fly look more realistic, add essential weight to the fly, and even create an enticing disturbance in the water.

### How to Tie In Bead Chain, Dumbbell, and Molded Plastic Eyes

1 Make several turns of thread around hook shank to form base. Snip a two-bead section from chain. Position section at desired location on hook.

2 Tie in bead-chain section with several turns of thread in a figure-eight pattern until secure. Add a drop of glue, if desired.

### How to Attach Doll Eye

1 Apply a small dab of epoxy to the back of the doll eye.

2 Press eye into position and hold or brace until set.

## How to Attach Burnt Monofilament Eyes

1 Select a length of 20- to 100-pound-test mono. Cut into two pieces. Melt ends with flame until a small bead forms. Allow to cool.

2 Tie in mono strands on either side of hook shank with soft loops and secure. Add a drop of super glue or epoxy, if desired.

## How to attach Hair Brush Eyes

1 Snip two bristles from a standard hairbrush. Flatten ends with pliers to make them easier to tie in with thread.

2 Tie in bristles on either side of hook shank with soft loops and secure. Add a drop of super glue or epoxy, if desired.

## How to Attach Adhesive Eyes

1 Bend eye to proper shape. Peel off backing and press into place.

## How To Apply Painted Eyes

1 Apply first color with a small brush. Allow color to dry completely. Add a small spot of black for pupil. Coat eye with clear epoxy or head cement, if desired.

## Braided Tube Bodies

Braided Mylar or mono tubing is an effective material for tying minnow and other saltwater fly patterns. It is flexible, easy to work with, can be colored with markers and resembles the scales of the natural baitfish. Mono tubing expands and contracts more easily than Mylar, and is more durable as well. Translucent tubing allows the underbody color to show through the finished body.

*This 'Cuda Fly has a braided tube body tied extended-body style.*

### *How to Tie In a Braided Tube Body, Baitfish-style*

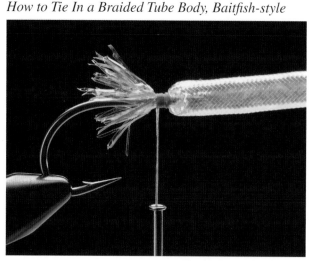

1 Cut a 2- to 3-inch section of body tubing. Slip one end over the hook eye. Tie in behind eye and make several half-hitches to secure. Trim thread and add a drop of super glue to secure.

2 Push tubing back over itself and hook shank to hook bend. Secure with several thread wraps and whip-finish. Trim excess tubing. Add a drop of super glue to secure.

### *How to Tie In a Braided Tube Body, Extended-body Style*

1 Push hook eye through tubing about a hook-shank length from end of tube material.

2 Make several turns of thread to secure. Whip finish. Add a drop of super glue or epoxy to secure.

## Epoxy Bodies

Epoxy has revolutionized saltwater fly tying. Epoxy bodies are more durable than braided tube bodies, allow the underbody to show through, and create a convincing realism.

For tying only a few flies, use a five-minute type epoxy. For tying more flies or when working more slowly, choose a slower-drying epoxy.

*The Goddard Mylar Minnow has a clear epoxy body.*

### How to Make an Epoxy Body

1 Tie in the underbody material according to the fly pattern recipe.

2 Mix the desired amount of epoxy.

3 Apply a thin coat of epoxy. Allow to dry completely. Adding a second coat too soon may cause epoxy to become cloudy.

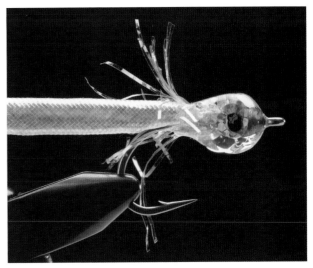

4 Apply a second coat. Keep fly moving until dry, if possible, to prevent drips and deformation.

*Strands of rug yarn make up the body on this Carpet Crab fly.*

## Crab Bodies

One of the most prized and toughest-fighting saltwater gamefish is the permit, but few fly anglers ever hooked one until the development of the crab fly. Below are two simple techniques for creating crab bodies.

### How to Tie a Yarn Crab Body

1 Tie in a strand of 2-inch stiff olive rug yarn. Continue tying in strands of rug yarn, alternating olive and tan colors.

2 Trim yarn strands to a crab shape. Coat yarn with five-minute-type epoxy, if desired.

### How to Make an Adhesive-pad Crab Body

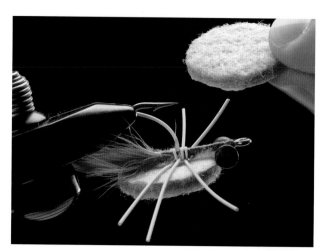

1 Tie in weight, eyes, tail and leg material according to recipe. Press adhesive Velcro or furniture pad material to top of hook.

2 Turn fly over. Press a second adhesive pad to bottom of fly. Color body and legs with markers, if desired.

## Tarpon-style Bodies

The "silver king" of saltwater gamefish is the magnificent tarpon. Flies tied for tarpon are based on the thin profile of the sleek needlefish, a staple in the tarpon's diet. Some tarpon flies call for painted or adhesive eyes to complete the illusion.

*The body of this fly is thread wrapped tarpon-style.*

*How to Tie a Tarpon-style Body*

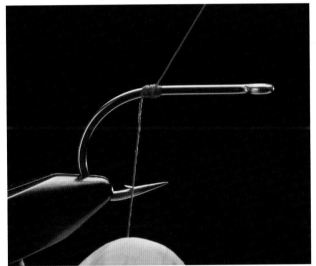

1 Begin thread at the place near the hook bend where the hackle tips are secured, according to the fly recipe.

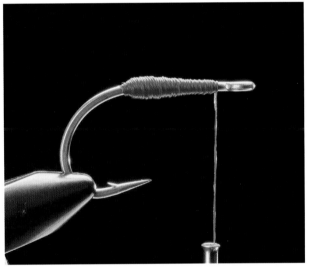

2 Wrap thread forward in neat turns, building a smooth body, to a point approximately ⅛ inch behind hook eye.

3 Make several whip finish knots and trim excess thread.

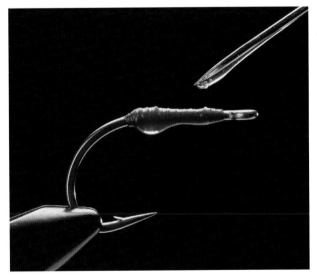

4 Apply a thin layer of epoxy or similar coating. Apply eyes, if desired.

# Finishing Knots

Before you trim off the thread and remove the fly from the vise, you must secure the thread using either a half-hitch or a whip-finish knot. The half-hitch is easier to learn but the whip-finish knot will last longer. Most flytiers use a special tool for the whip-finish knot, but you can easily tie a half-hitch without any special tools, as shown below (bare hook used for demonstration purposes).

*How to Tie a Half-hitch Finishing Knot*

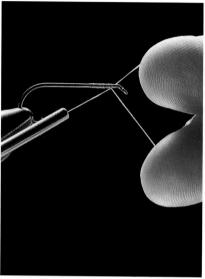

1 Hold bobbin in left hand with 6 to 8 inches of thread between bobbin and hook eye. Spread first and second fingers of right hand, and place them against thread with palm facing away from you.

2 Twist right hand as you raise bobbin, forming a loop. Keep thread against fingertips, so palm is facing toward you and bobbin is horizontal.

3 Begin to raise loop, hooking the thread beneath hook eye. Remove second finger from loop.

4 Raise loop over head of fly. Carefully remove first finger.

5 Slowly close loop by pulling down on bobbin. Repeat steps 1 through 5 several times. Trim excess thread.

6 Apply a small amount of head cement to completed half-hitches for added strength.

*How to Use a Whip-finish Tool*

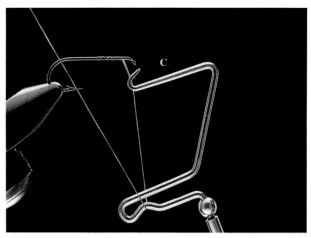

1 Hold bobbin in left hand with 6 to 8 inches of thread between bobbin and hook eye. Place bend of tool (A) against thread. Raise bobbin to position (B).

2 Catch thread with hook of tool (C) as shown.

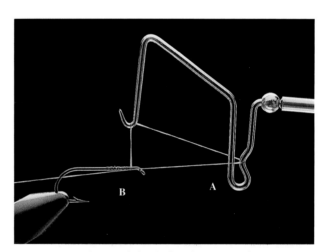

3 Lift handle to the right and rotate tool 180 degrees, keeping tension on thread. The thread (A to B) should be nearly parallel to shank.

4 Rotate tool around shank five times, trapping thread (A to B) against shank.

5 Raise tool above shank to free thread from bend (A). Do not release tension on thread.

6 Pull bobbin slowly to close thread loop. Remove tool from thread and tug on bobbin to tighten knot. Trim excess thread and apply head cement to knot. The tag end is now covered with wraps, making the knot very secure.

# Fly Patterns

Once you have learned to tie the basic parts of a fly — tail, body, wings and hackle — you can combine them to create a complete pattern. But first you should know how to read a fly-pattern recipe.

Any chef will tell you that the first ingredient listed in a recipe is the first to go into the dish. A fly-pattern recipe is no different.

The fly recipes in this book (sample below) begin with (1) hook, including manufacturer and model number, although you can substitute many other similar hooks. The size designation after the semicolon lists the size range in which the pattern is most commonly tied. The (2) thread listing gives you the recommended thread color and size. The recipe also lists the fly parts, such as (3) wing, (4) tail, (5) body and (6) hackle, in the order in which they are tied in.

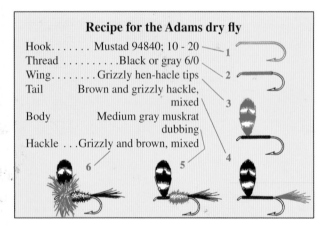

**Recipe for the Adams dry fly**

Hook. . . . . . . Mustad 94840; 10 - 20
Thread . . . . . . . . . Black or gray 6/0
Wing. . . . . . . . Grizzly hen-hacle tips
Tail      Brown and grizzly hackle, mixed
Body      Medium gray muskrat dubbing
Hackle . . . Grizzly and brown, mixed

In this section, you will learn to tie the seven basic patterns, including a streamer, a nymph, a dry fly, a wet fly, a terrestrial, a bass fly and a saltwater fly. Following the instructions for each basic pattern are several pages showing recipes for many other flies of the same type.

Keep in mind that many popular fly patterns are tied in different fly types. In the fly catalogs that follow, for instance, you'll find recipes for a March Brown in dry-fly, wet-fly and nymph versions. You'll even find variations in materials and elements used in a specific pattern, depending on the region and flytier. A Light Cahill *wet* fly can be tied with a tail of duck flank or hackle fibers; the Light Cahill *dry* can be tied with an upright-and-divided hackle-fiber wing, or a parachute-style hair wing.

# Streamers

A streamer is designed to imitate a baitfish rather than an insect. Traditional streamers have hackle-feather wings that extend back, or "stream," over the body of the fly.

Another popular type of streamer is the *bucktail*, which has hair wings, making it more durable.

Both types can be extremely productive for salmon, trout, steelhead, bass and even pike.

Some streamer patterns, called imitators, closely resemble a real baitfish. Others, called attractors, use flash, color and movement to draw a strike.

Streamers are generally tied on extra-long hooks to help give them the long profile of a baitfish.

Streamers and bucktails are often weighted with lead wire, and are fished deep by casting them with a weighted line, or trolling.

Streamers can be retrieved upstream or down, or across the current with a jerky, twitching retrieve to simulate a baitfish.

POPULAR HOOKS include: (1) TMC 5263; (2) Mustad 9672, (3) 9049X and (4) 79580.

Fly-tying courses often begin with a streamer or bucktail pattern. Their large size and simple construction make these patterns easy to tie.

Many fly anglers believe that eyes increase the effectiveness of a streamer. Dab on eyes with a small dowel dipped in white acrylic paint. Use a smaller dowel to dab on the black pupil.

One classic, but still popular and effective, bucktail pattern is the Mickey Finn (below). Designed by John Alden Knight in the 1930s, it was named for the infamous drugged drink.

The Mickey Finn is an excellent baitfish imitation. The red stripe of bucktail resembles the lateral line of a small minnow or trout. Instructions for tying the Mickey Finn are on the following pages.

BUILD a mound of thread, if needed, just behind the eye. The eye of some streamer hooks is slightly open; without a mound, materials could slip into, or snag on, the eye.

*The Mickey Finn bucktail*

PAINT ON eyes, then dip the head into clear gloss lacquer. After lacquer dries, clean hook eye with dubbing needle.

## How to Tie a Streamer: the Mickey Finn

| Recipe | |
|---|---|
| Hook | Mustad 9672; 2 - 12 |
| Thread | Black 3/0 |
| Weight (optional) | Fine lead wire |
| Ribbing | Oval silver tinsel |
| Body | Flat silver tinsel |
| Wing | Yellow and red bucktail, or calf tail |

### How to Tie the Mickey Finn

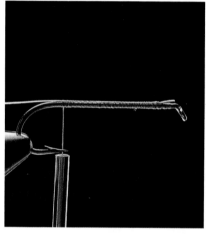

1 Tie in a 4-inch length of oval silver tinsel ribbing on top of hook shank, starting thread just behind hook eye and wrapping back to bend to secure tinsel.

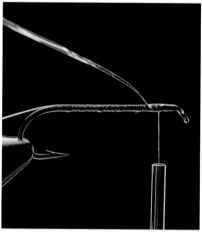

2 Wind thread forward again to tie-in point behind hook eye. Tie in a 6-inch length of flat silver tinsel body material.

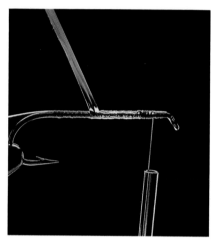

3 Wrap flat tinsel back to bend of hook. Each wrap should touch prevous wrap so there are no gaps.

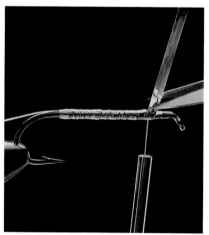

4 Reverse direction and wrap tinsel forward to tie-in point, overlapping first layer. Secure with several turns of thread.

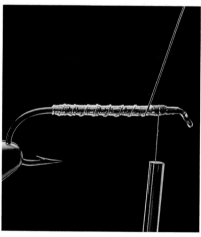

5 Wrap ribbing on hook, starting near bend, and wrap forward.

6 Cut a small bundle of yellow bucktail, and another of red. Comb out underfur with dubbing needle.

7 Stack bucktail fibers to align tips. Divide yellow bucktail into two equal bundles.

8 Measure first bundle to approximately 1½ times hook-shank length.

9 Tie in first bundle of yellow bucktail with several soft loops. Apply moderate thread tension for first few wraps, then increase tension for several more wraps. If you are having problems getting bucktail to stay on top of hook, reduce amount of bucktail.

10 Trim butt ends of bucktail at an upward angle, as shown; then wrap thread forward to cover tapered ends.

11 Measure bundle of red bucktail to same length as first yellow bundle and place it directly on top of yellow bundle. Tie in as in steps 9 and 10.

12 Measure second bundle of yellow to same length as first and tie in as in steps 9 and 10. Whip-finish, and apply head cement.

# Catalog of Streamers

### Black-nosed Dace

Hook . . . . . . . . . . . . . . . . . . Mustad 9672; 4-12
Thread . . . . . . . . . . . . . . . . . . . . . . . Black 6/0
Tail . . . . . . . . . . . . . . . . . . . . . . . . . Red yarn
Rib . . . . . . . . . . . . . . . . . . . Oval silver tinsel
Body . . . . . . . . . . . . . . . . . . . Flat silver tinsel
Wing . . . . . . . . . . . . . . Brown over black over
white bucktail

### Royal Coachman Bucktail

Hook . . . . . . . . . . . . . . . . Mustad 3666; 10-16
Thread . . . . . . . . . . . . . . . . . . . . . . . Black 6/0
Tail . . . . . . . . . . Golden pheasant tippet
Rib . . . . . . . . . . . . . . . . . . . . . Fine gold wire
Butt . . . . . . . . . . . . . . . . . . . . . . Peacock herl
Body . . . . . . . . . . . . . . . . . . . . . . . . Red floss
Thorax . . . . . . . . . . . . . . . . . . . . . Peacock herl
Hackle . . . . . . . . . . . . . . . . Dark brown hen
Wing . . . . . . . . . . . . . . . . . . . . White bucktail

### Llama

Hook . . . . . . . . . . . . . . . . . . Mustad 9672; 4-10
Thread . . . . . . . . . . . . . . . . . . . . . . . Black 6/0
Rib . . . . . . . . . . . . . . . . . . . . Oval gold tinsel
Body . . . . . . . . . . . . . . . . . . . Red wool yarn
Wing . . . . . . . . . . . . . . . . . . Woodchuck hair
Hackle . . . . . . . . . . . . . . . . . . . . . Grizzly hen

### Light Spruce

Hook . . . . . . . . . . . . . . . . . Mustad 9672; 2-10
Thread . . . . . . . . . . . . . . . . . . . . . . . Black 6/0
Tail . . . . . . . . . . . . . . . . Peacock sword fibers
Rib . . . . . . . . . . . . . . . . . . . . Fine copper wire
Body . . . . . . . . . . . . . . Rear half red wool yarn,
front half peacock herl
Wing . . . . . . Two badger-colored saddle hackles
Hackle . . . . . . . . . . . . . . . . . . . Badger saddle

### Silver Darter

Hook . . . . . . . . . . . . . . . . . Mustad 9672; 4-10
Thread . . . . . . . . . . . . . . . . . . . . . . . Black 6/0
Tag . . . . . . . . . Red monocord, to secure end of
body tubing
Body . . . . . . . . . . . . . Silver Mylar body tubing
Beard . . . . . . . . . . . . . . . Peacock sword fibers
Wing . . . . . . . . . . . . . . . . . . . . Badger saddle

### Pass Lake

Hook . . . . . . . . . . . . . . . . . . Mustad 9672; 8-12
Thread . . . . . . . . . . . . . . . . . . . . . . . Black 6/0
Tail . . . . . . . . . . . . Brown hen hackle fibers
Body . . . . . . . . . . . . . . . . . . . Black chenille
Hackle . . . . . . . . . . . . . . . . . . . . . Brown hen
Wing . . . . . . . . . . . . . . . . . . . . White calf tail

### Grizzly King

Hook . . . . . . . . . . . . . . . . . . Mustad 9672; 4-12
Thread . . . . . . . . . . . . . . . . . . . . . . . Black 6/0
Tail . . . . . . . . . . . . . . . . . . Red hackle fibers
Rib . . . . . . . . . . . . . . . . Fine flat silver tinsel
Body . . . . . . . . . . . . . . . . . . . . . . . Green floss
Beard . . . . . . . . . . Grizzly or dun hackle fibers
Wing . . . . . . . . . . . . . . . . . . . . Grizzly saddle

### Black Matuka

Hook . . . . . . . . . . . . . . . . . Mustad 9672; 2-10
Thread . . . . . . . . . . . . . . . . . . . . . . . Black 6/0
Rib . . . . . . . . . . . . . . . . . . . . Fine copper wire
Body . . . . . . . . . . . . . . . . . . . Black chenille
Wing . . . . . Four black hen saddle hackles, tied
down over body with rib
Hackle . . . . . . . . . . . . . . . . . . . . . . . Black hen

### Byford's White Zonker

Hook . . . . . . . . . . . . . . . . . . Mustad 9672; 2-6
Thread . . . . . . . . . . . . . . . . . . . . . . . White 6/0
Weight . . . . . . . . . . . . . . . . . . . . . . Lead wire
Body . . . . . . . . . . . . Pearl Mylar body tubing
Wing and Tail . . . . . . . . . . . . White rabbit strip,
glued to body
Topping . . . . . . . . . . . . . . Pearl Krystal Flash
Beard . . . . . . . . . . . . . . White rabbit dubbing
Eyes . . . . . . . . Painted yellow with black pupil

## Gray Ghost

| | |
|---|---|
| Hook | Mustad 79580; 2-10 |
| Thread | Black 6/0 |
| Tag and Rib | Strand of fine flat silver tinsel |
| Body | Orange floss |
| Beard | Four strands of peacock herl, white, bucktail, golden pheasant crest |
| Underwing | Golden pheasant crest |
| Wing | Four gray dun saddle hackles |
| Sides | Two silver pheasant body feathers |
| Cheeks | Jungle cock (optional) |

## Black Ghost

| | |
|---|---|
| Hook | Mustad 79580; 2-6 |
| Thread | Black 6/0 |
| Tail | Yellow hackle fibers |
| Rib | Medium flat silver tinsel |
| Body | Black floss |
| Beard | Yellow hackle fibers |
| Wing | Four white saddle hackles |
| Cheeks | Jungle cock (optional) |

## Supervisor

| | |
|---|---|
| Hook | Mustad 79580; 2-10 |
| Thread | Black 6/0 |
| Tail | Red wool yarn, short |
| Rib | Medium oval silver tinsel |
| Body | Flat silver tinsel |
| Beard | White hackle fibers |
| Wing | White bucktail with four blue saddle hackles |
| Sides | Two green saddle hackles |
| Topping | Peacock herl |
| Cheeks | Jungle cock (optional) |

## Purple Woolly Bugger

| | |
|---|---|
| Hook | Mustad 9672; 2-12 |
| Thread | Black 6/0 |
| Tail | Purple marabou |
| Rib | Fine copper wire (optional) |
| Body | Purple chenille |
| Hackle | Black, palmered over body |

## Lead-eyed Egg Leech

| | |
|---|---|
| Hook | Mustad 9672; 4-8 |
| Thread | Black 6/0 |
| Tail | Black rabbit fur strip |
| Body | Black rabbit fur strip, wrapped |
| Eyes | Nickel-plated hourglass eyes |
| Thorax | Black rabbit dubbing |
| Head | Fluorescent hot pink chenille |

## Muddler Minnow

| | |
|---|---|
| Hook | Mustad 9672; 2-14 |
| Thread | Black 6/0 |
| Tail | Mottled turkey wing quill segment |
| Body | Gold tinsel |
| Underwing | Gray squirrel tail |
| Wing | Mottled turkey quill |
| Collar | Natural deer hair, spun |
| Head | Natural deer hair, spun and clipped |

## Black Marabou Muddler

| | |
|---|---|
| Hook | Mustad 9672; 2-10 |
| Thread | Black 6/0 |
| Tail | Red hackle fibers |
| Body | Silver tinsel |
| Wing | Black marabou with six strands of peacock herl |
| Collar | Deer hair, spun |
| Head | Deer hair, spun and clipped |

## Olive Whit's Sculpin

| | |
|---|---|
| Hook | Mustad 9672; 1/0-8 |
| Thread | Olive 3/0 |
| Rib | Medium oval gold tinsel |
| Body | Light olive wool yarn |
| Thorax | Red wool dubbing |
| Wing | Two olive grizzly hackles, tied to body with ribbing |
| Fins | Olive hen mallard breast |
| Collar | Olive deer hair, spun and clipped |
| Head | Olive deer hair with a band of black deer hair, spun and clipped |

## Wool Shad

| | |
|---|---|
| Hook | TMC 5263; 2-10 |
| Thread | Gray 3/0 |
| Wing | Silver Krystal Flash over white marabou |
| Sides | Grizzly saddle hackles, splayed |
| Body | Gray thread |
| Collar | Grizzly saddle hackle |
| Head | Wool dubbing, clipped to shape |
| Eyes | Hourglass eyes, white with black pupils |

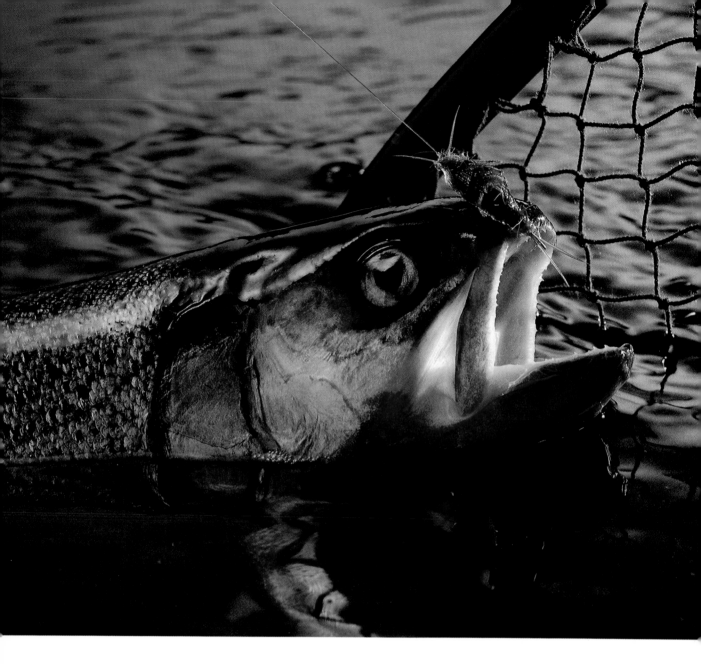

# Nymphs

Nymphs make up the second largest fly-pattern category, next to dry flies, and are an important part of any flytier's repertoire.

Anglers use the term "nymph" when referring to any of the larval, pupal and nymphal stages of aquatic insects. In fly tying, the term refers to imitations of these forms, or to imitations of crustaceans, such as scuds, shrimp and sometimes crayfish.

Nymphs are effective not only for trout, but also for panfish and bass. With immature aquatic insects and crustaceans making up a significant portion of the diet of most gamefish, as much as 90 percent in the case of trout, it's not surprising that nymphs work so well.

Designed to be fished below the surface, a nymph is usually tied on a hook that is slightly heavier than a dry-fly hook, and is often productive even when fish do not appear to be feeding.

Not all nymph patterns are exact imitations. Some, called searching patterns, are impressionistic, suggesting a number of food items rather than a specific

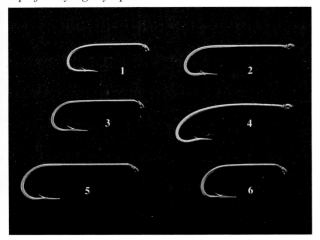

POPULAR HOOKS include: (1) TMC 3761, (2) TMC 939S, (3) Mustad 9671, (4) TMC 200R, (5) Mustad 9672 and (6) Mustad 3906.

ADD weight to center of hook shank to make fly sink horizontally.

APPLY a few drops of head cement to wingcase feather to keep fibers together on completed wingcase.

DUB thorax thicker than abdomen to create a realistic profile and provide enough material for plucking out legs.

one. These patterns are a good choice when it is difficult to determine exactly which naturals the fish are eating.

Nymph patterns range in size from tiny imitations of midge larvae to large stonefly patterns. They can be tied using natural and synthetic materials in a variety of colors, shapes and sizes, depending on the naturals.

Nymphs should be fished at the depth that fish are taking the naturals. When fish are feeding deep, use a weighted nymph or add a split shot to your leader a few feet from the fly. Use an unweighted nymph for fishing just below the surface.

One of the most popular and effective nymphs is the Gold-ribbed Hare's Ear (right and following pages). Its general profile and color are similar to many different species of mayfly, making it an excellent

searching pattern all season long. Weight the pattern, if desired, with lead wire or a brass bead (p. 42).

The Hare's Ear gets its unusual name from the soft, absorbent fibers of a hare's mask (p. 25), used for the body and tail of the fly.

*The Gold-ribbed Hare's Ear nymph*

# How to Tie a Nymph: The Gold-ribbed Hare's Ear

| Recipe | |
|---|---|
| Hook . . . . . . . . . | Mustad 3906; 8 - 16 |
| Thread . . . . . . . . . | Tan or brown 6/0 |
| Tail. . . . | Hare's mask guard hairs, or brown hackle fibers |
| Rib . . . . . . . | Fine oval gold tinsel, or copper wire |
| Body . . . . . . . | Hare's mask dubbing, thorax thicker than abdomen |
| Wingcase . . . . . . . | Mottled turkey, or goose wing-quill segment |

## *How to Tie a Gold-ribbed Hare's Ear Nymph*

**1** Start thread at midpoint of hook shank and wind back to bend. Tie in 10 to 15 hare's mask fibers at bend to form tail. Wind thread forward to middle of shank and trim any excess butts.

**2** Tie in a two-inch length of fine oval gold tinsel ribbing and wrap thread over tinsel to hook bend. Trim off any tinsel that extends forward.

**3** Apply hare's mask dubbing to thread.

**4** Wind the dubbed thread forward to middle of shank to form tapered body.

**5** Wrap tinsel forward to middle of shank with four or five open-spiral turns. Secure with several turns of thread, and trim off tag end of tinsel.

**6** Snip a ½-inch-wide quill segment from a large mottled turkey or goose wing feather for wingcase.

**7** Tie in quill segment, shiny side up, with tip toward bend. Make several turns of thread to secure.

**8** Snip off butt end of segment, then wind thread forward over trimmed end to secure. Wind thread back to wing tie-in point.

**9** Apply a generous amount of hare's mask dubbing to thread, then wind dubbed thread forward to about one hook-eye length behind eye to form thorax.

**10** Pull end of quill segment over thorax to form wingcase. Secure wingcase with several turns of thread, and trim excess. Form head, whip-finish and apply head cement to knot and wingcase. Pluck out fibers from thorax, if desired, to form legs.

# Catalog of Nymphs

### Pheasant Tail Nymph

Hook................. Mustad 9671; 10-18
Thread....................... Brown 6/0
Tail..................... Pheasant tail fibers
Rib..................... Fine copper wire
Body... Pheasant tail fibers, wrapped herl-style
Wingcase.............. Pheasant tail fibers
Thorax.................... Peacock herl

### Breadcrust

Hook................. Mustad 3906; 8-14
Thread....................... Black 6/0
Rib........ Stripped ruffed grouse tail feather,
and fine copper wire
Body.......... Burnt orange rabbit dubbing
Hackle..................... Grizzly hen

### Dark Hendrickson Nymph

Hook................. Mustad 9671; 10-18
Thread........................ Olive 6/0
Tail.............. Lemon wood duck fibers
Rib...................... Brown floss
Abdomen.................. Red fox dubbing
Wingcase....... White-tip turkey tail segment
Thorax.................. Red fox dubbing
Sides................... Brown partridge

### Blue-wing Olive Nymph

Hook................. Mustad 9671; 14-18
Thread........................ Olive 6/0
Tail.......... Lemon wood duck flank fibers
Rib...................... Brown silk thread
Body.......... Medium olive rabbit dubbing
Wingcase.......... Goose wing quill fibers
Thorax......... Medium olive rabbit dubbing
Legs......... Brown partridge hackle fibers

### Isonychia Nymph

Hook................. Mustad 9671; 10-16
Thread........................ Red 6/0
Tail................... Pheasant tail fibers
Shellback..... Stripped white hackle stem over
top of body and wingcase, tied in with rib
Rib...................... Black floss
Body.............. Dark red-brown dubbing
Wingcase.............. Dark quill segment
Thorax............. Dark red-brown dubbing
Sides.............. Wood duck flank fibers

### Quill Gordon Nymph

Hook................. Mustad 9671; 10-14
Thread........................ Olive 6/0
Tail.............. Two pheasant tail fibers
Rib...................... Brown thread
Body.................... Beaver dubbing
Wingcase.......... Mottled turkey wing quill
Thorax................... Beaver dubbing
Beard.............. Brown partridge fibers

### Black Quill Nymph

Hook................. Mustad 9671; 10-14
Thread........................ Black 6/0
Tail.............. Medium dun hackle fibers
Body.............. Stripped peacock herl
Wingcase.... Dark mallard wing-quill segment
Thorax................... Muskrat dubbing
Beard.............. Medium blue dun hen

### Red Squirrel Nymph

Hook................. Mustad 9672; 6-10
Thread........................ Black 6/0
Tail................ Hare's mask guard hair
Body.............. Red squirrel dubbing
Rib................ Fine oval gold tinsel
Thorax.......... Dark gray Antron dubbing

### March Brown Nymph

Hook................. Mustad 9671; 12-18
Thread........................ Rust 6/0
Tail................... Pheasant tail fibers
Rib...................... Brown thread
Body........ Red fox and amber goat dubbing
Wingcase....... Mottled turkey quill segment
Thorax...... Red fox and amber goat dubbing
Sides................... Partridge hackle

### Flashabou Nymph

Hook . . . . . . . . . . . . . . Mustad 3906B; 10-18
Thread . . . . . . . . . . . . . . . . . . . . Black 6/0
Tail. . . . . . . . . . . Ringneck pheasant tail fibers
Body . . . . . . . . . . . Pearl Flashabou, wrapped
Wingcase. . . . . . . . . . . . . . . . Pearl Flashabou
Thorax . . . . . . . . Black rabbit and goat dubbing

### Prince Nymph

Hook. . . . . . . . . . . . . . Mustad 9671; 4-10
Thread . . . . . . . . . . . . . . . . . . . . Black 6/0
Tail . . . . . . . . . . . . . . . . . Brown goose biots
Rib . . . . . . . . . . . . . . . . Fine flat gold tinsel
Body . . . . . . . . . . . . . . . . . . . . Peacock herl
Hackle . . . . . . . . . . . . . . . . . . . . . Brown
Wing . . . . . . . . . . . White biots tied in with tips
facing back

### Tellico Nymph

Hook . . . . . . . . . . . . . . Mustad 9671; 12-16
Thread . . . . . . . . . . . . . . . . . . . . Black 6/0
Tail. . . . . . . . . . . . . . . . . Guinea body fibers
Shellback . . . . . . . Ringneck pheasant tail fibers
Rib . . . . . . . . . . . . . . . . . . . . Peacock herl
Body . . . . . . . . . . . . . . . . . . . Yellow floss
Hackle . . . . . . . . . . . . Furnace-colored hackle

### Zug Bug

Hook . . . . . . . . . . . . . . . Mustad 9671; 8-16
Thread . . . . . . . . . . . . . . . . . . . . Black 6/0
Tail. . . . . . . . . . . . . . . . Peacock sword fibers
Body . . . . . . . . . . . . . . . . . . . . Peacock herl
Hackle . . . . . . . . . . . . . Brown, wet-fly style
Wingcase . . . . . . . . . . . Lemon wood duck flank

### Montana Stone

Hook. . . . . . . . . . . . . . . . Mustad 9672; 6-10
Thread . . . . . . . . . . . . . . . . . . . . Black 6/0
Tail . . . . . . . . . . . . . . . . . Brown goose biots
Body . . . . . . . . . . . . . . . . . Brown chenille
Wingcase . . . . . . . . . . . . . . . Brown chenille
Thorax . . . . . . . . . . . . . . . . Orange chenille
Hackle . . . . . . . . Black, palmered over thorax

### Bitch Creek

Hook . . . . . . . . . . . . . . . Mustad 9672; 2-10
Thread . . . . . . . . . . . . . . . . . . . . Black 6/0
Tail. . . . . . . . . . . . . . . . . White rubber strips
Body . . . . . . . . . . . Black and orange chenille
Rib . . . . . . . . . . . Fine gold wire, over thorax
Thorax . . . . . . . . . . . . . . . . . . Black chenille
Hackle . . . . . . . . Brown, palmered over thorax
Antennae . . . . . . . . . . . . . . White rubber strips

### Damselfly Nymph

Hook . . . . . . . . . . . . . . . Mustad 9672; 8-12
Thread . . . . . . . . . . . . . . . . . . . . Olive 6/0
Tail. . . . . . . . . . . . . . . . . . . Olive marabou
Body . . . . . . . . . . . . . Green yarn or dubbing
Rib. . . . . . . . . . . . . . . . . . Oval gold tinsel
Eyes. . . . . . . . . . . . . . . . . . Black hourglass
Thorax and Head. . . . . . Green yarn or dubbing
Sides . . . . . . . . . . . . . . . . Green grizzly hen
Wingcase . . . . . . . . . Olive Swiss Straw, folded

### Green Drake Nymph

Hook. . . . . . . . . . . . . . . . Mustad 9672; 10-12
Thread . . . . . . . . . . . . . . . . . . . . Olive 6/0
Tail . . . . Mahogany ringneck pheasant tail fibers
Rib . . . . . . . . . . . . . . . . . . . . . Olive floss
Abdomen . . . . . . . . . . . . . . . Olive-tan dubbing
Wingcase . . . . . . . White-tip turkey tail segment
Thorax . . . . . . . . . . . . . . . . . Olive-tan dubbing
Sides . . . . . . . . . . . . . Lemon wood duck fibers

### Hexagenia Nymph

Hook . . . . . . . . . . . . . . . Mustad 9672; 4-10
Thread . . . . . . . . . . . . . . . . . . . . Olive 6/0
Tail. . . . . . . . . . . . . . . . Barred olive marabou
Rib. . . . . . . . . . . . . . . . . Fine copper wire
Body . . . . . . . . . . . . . Medium brown dubbing
Wingcase . . . . . . . . . . . . . . . Mottled turkey
Thorax . . . . . . . . . . . . Medium brown dubbing
Legs. . . . . . . . . . . . . . . . Barred olive marabou
Eyes. . . . . . . . . . . . . . . . . . . Monofilament
Antennae . . . . . . . . . . . Barred olive marabou

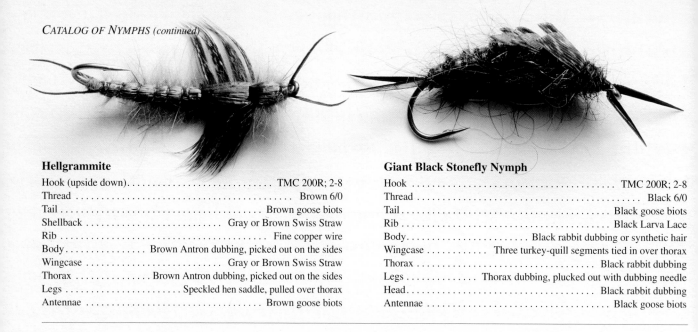

### Hellgrammite

| | |
|---|---|
| Hook (upside down) | TMC 200R; 2-8 |
| Thread | Brown 6/0 |
| Tail | Brown goose biots |
| Shellback | Gray or Brown Swiss Straw |
| Rib | Fine copper wire |
| Body | Brown Antron dubbing, picked out on the sides |
| Wingcase | Gray or Brown Swiss Straw |
| Thorax | Brown Antron dubbing, picked out on the sides |
| Legs | Speckled hen saddle, pulled over thorax |
| Antennae | Brown goose biots |

### Giant Black Stonefly Nymph

| | |
|---|---|
| Hook | TMC 200R; 2-8 |
| Thread | Black 6/0 |
| Tail | Black goose biots |
| Rib | Black Larva Lace |
| Body | Black rabbit dubbing or synthetic hair |
| Wingcase | Three turkey-quill segments tied in over thorax |
| Thorax | Black rabbit dubbing |
| Legs | Thorax dubbing, plucked out with dubbing needle |
| Head | Black rabbit dubbing |
| Antennae | Black goose biots |

### Brassie

| | |
|---|---|
| Hook | TMC 200R; 10-18 |
| Thread | Black 6/0 |
| Body | Copper wire |
| Thorax | Gray muskrat dubbing, with guard hairs |

### Peacock Larva

| | |
|---|---|
| Hook | Mustad 3906; 12-16 |
| Thread | Black 6/0 |
| Rib | Fine copper wire, through body and thorax |
| Body | Bright green yarn |
| Thorax | Peacock herl |
| Beard | Two short strands of peacock herl |

### Peeking Caddis

| | |
|---|---|
| Hook | Mustad 3906; 12-16 |
| Thread | Black 6/0 |
| Rib | Fine oval gold tinsel |
| Body | Natural rabbit dubbing |
| Thorax | Olive rabbit dubbing |
| Beard | Ringneck pheasant back fibers |
| Head | Black ostrich herl |

### Olive Larva

| | |
|---|---|
| Hook | TMC 200R; 12-16 |
| Thread | Brown 6/0 |
| Rib | Fine gold wire |
| Body | Olive dubbing |
| Beard | Brown partridge hackle |
| Head | Dark brown rabbit dubbing |

### Speckled Sedge

| | |
|---|---|
| Hook | Mustad 3906; 12-16 |
| Thread | Brown 6/0 |
| Rib | Reddish brown Australian opossum, tightly dubbed onto thread to make ribbing |
| Body | Light brown mink dubbing |
| Wing | Gray duck wing-quill segments |
| Beard | Brown partridge hackle |
| Head | Dark brown rabbit dubbing |

### Olive Sedge

| | |
|---|---|
| Hook | Mustad 3906; 14-18 |
| Thread | Brown 6/0 |
| Body | Pale olive dubbing |
| Wingcase | Natural gray duck-quill segments |
| Beard | Brown partridge hackle |
| Head | Dark brown rabbit dubbing |

### GLF Cased Caddis

Hook . . . . . . . . . . . . . . . . . . . . TMC 100; 8-14
Thread . . . . . . . . . . . . . . . . . . . . . . Brown 6/0
Body . . . . Dark brown and gray grouse hackles
wrapped herl-style, clipped
Thorax . . . . . . . . . . . . . Pale olive rabbit dubbing
Beard . . . . . Dark brown and gray hackle fibers
Head . . . . . . . . . . . . . Black dubbing (optional)

### GLF Emerging Caddis

Hook . . . . . . . . . . . . . . . . . . . TMC 100; 12-18
Thread . . . . . . . . . . . . . . . . . . . . . . Black 6/0
Tail . . . . . . . . . . . . . . Antron fibers from body
Underbody . . . . . . . . Gold Antron dubbing and
brown rabbit dubbing
Body . . . . . . . . . . . . . . . . . . Tan Antron yarn
Wing . . . . . . . . . . . . . Dark speckled deer hair
Head . . . . . . . . . . . . . . . Brown rabbit dubbing

### Deep Sparkling Pupa

Hook . . . . . . . . . . . . . . . . . . . TMC 100; 12-18
Thread . . . . . . . . . . . . . . . . . . . . . . Black 6/0
Underbody . . . . . One-half olive, one-half bright
green Antron
Body . . . . . . . . . . . . Medium olive Antron yarn
Hackle . . . . . . . . . . . . . . . . . . . . . . . . Grouse

### Goplin Emerger

Hook . . . . . . . . . . . . . . . . . . . TMC 100; 12-20
Thread . . . . . . . . . . . . . . . . . . . . . . Brown 6/0
Tail . . . . . . . . . . . . . . . . . Brown hackle fibers
Body . . . . . . . . . . . . . . . . . . . . . Tan dubbing
Wingcase . . . . . . Gray hen-hackle fibers, tied to
form loop
Legs . . . . . Gray hen-hackle fibers cut from loop,
each side
Thorax . . . . . . . . . . . . . . . . . . . . Tan dubbing

### Floating Nymph

Hook . . . . . . . . . . . . . . . . . . . TMC 100; 12-20
Thread . . . . . . . . . . . . . . . . . . . . . . Olive 6/0
Tail . . . . . . . . . . . . . . . . . . Dun hackle fibers
Rib . . . . . . . . . . . . . . . . . . . . . . Tan thread
Body . . . . . . . . . . . . . . . . . . . . Olive dubbing
Wingcase . . . Brown dubbing spun onto thread,
then pushed down onto top
of thorax to form ball
Beard . . . . . . . . . . . . . . . . . . Dun hackle fibers

### CDC Hendrickson Emerger

Hook . . . . . . . . . . . . . . . . . . . TMC 100; 12-20
Thread . . . . . . . . . . . . . . . . . . . . . . Brown 6/0
Tail . . . . . . . . . . Lemon wood duck flank fibers
Rib . . . . . . . . . . . . . . . . . Fine copper wire
Body . . . . . . . . . . . . . . Brown Antron dubbing
Wing . . . . . . Dun CDC feathers, tied in at sides
Legs . . . . . . . . . . . . . . . . . . . Partridge hackle
Head . . . . . . . . . . . . . . . . . . . Brown Antron

### Olive Scud

Hook . . . . . . . . . . . . . . . . . . TMC 2457; 10-18
Thread . . . . . . . . . . . . . . . . . . . . . . Brown 6/0
Tail . . . . . . . . . . . . . . . . . . . Olive hackle fibers
Rib . . . . . . . . . . . . . . . . . . . . . . . Black thread
Body . . . . Mixed olive rabbit and goat dubbing,
picked out on bottom
Shellback . . . . . . . . . . . . . . . . . . . Clear plastic
Antennae . . . . . . . . . . . . . . . Olive hackle fibers

### Big Horn Scud

Hook . . . . . . . . . . . . . . . . . . Mustad 3906; 8-16
Thread . . . . . . . . . . . . . . . . . . . . . Orange 6/0
Tail . . . . . . . . . . Ringneck pheasant tail fibers
Rib . . . . . . . . . . . . . . . . . . . . . . Copper wire
Body . . . . . . . . . . . . . . Yellow Antron dubbing,
picked out on underside
Shellback . . . . . . . . . . . . . . . . . Clear plastic

### Sow Bug

Hook . . . . . . . . . . . . . . . . . Mustad 3906; 10-16
Thread . . . . . . . . . . . . . . . . . . . . . . Gray 6/0
Tail . . . . . . . . . . . . . . . . . . . Gray goose biots
Rib . . . . . . . . . . . . . . . . . . . . Fine silver wire
Body . . . . . . . . . . . . . . . . . . . Muskrat dubbing
Legs . . . . Fibers, picked out from body dubbing

### Bead-head Prince

Hook . . . . . . . . . . . . . . . . . . . TMC 3761; 8-16
Thread . . . . . . . . . . . . . . . . . . . . . . . . Red 6/0
Head . . . . . . . . . . . . . . . . . . . . . . . Brass bead
Tail . . . . . . . . . . . . . . . . Brown goose biots
Rib . . . . . . . . . . . . . . . . . . . . . . Gold Mylar
Body . . . . . . . . . . . . . . . . . . . . . Peacock herl
Wing . . . . . . . . . . . . . . . . . . White goose biots
Hackle . . . . . . . . . . . . . . . . . . . . Brown hen

### 2¹/₂-week Caddis

Hook . . . . . . . . . . . . . . . . . TMC 206BL; 14-18
Thread . . . . . . . . . . . . . . . . . . . . . . . Olive 6/0
Head . . . . . . . . . . . . . . . . . . . . . . . Brass bead
Body . . . . . . . Micro chenille, with singed end
Wing . . . . . . . . . . . . . . . . . . . . . . . . Tan CDC
Sides . . . . . . . . . . Mallard wing-quill segments
Thorax . . . . . . . . . . . . . . . . . . . . Peacock herl

### Bead-head Hare's Ear

Hook . . . . . . . . . . . . . . . . . . . TMC 3761; 10-18
Thread . . . . . . . . . . . . . . . . . . . . . . . Black 6/0
Head . . . . . . . . . . . . . . . . . . . . . . Copper bead
Tail . . . . . . . . . . . . . . . Hare's mask guard hair
Rib . . . . . . . . . . . . . . . . . . . Gold flat Mylar
Body . . . . . . . . . . . . . . . . Hare's mask dubbing
Legs . . . . . . . . . . . . . Hare's mask guard hair

### Bead-head Caddis Pupa

Hook . . . . . . . . . . . . . . . . . . TMC 3761; 10-18
Thread . . . . . . . . . . . . . . . . . . . . . . Olive 6/0
Head . . . . . . . . . . . . . . . . . . . . . . . Brass bead
Body . . . . . . . . . . . . . . . . Olive rabbit dubbing
Hackle . . . . . . . . . . . . . . . . . Brown partridge
Wing . . . . . . . . . Ringneck pheasant tail fibers

### Bead-head Pheasant Tail

Hook . . . . . . . . . . . . . . . . . . . TMC 2457; 10-18
Thread . . . . . . . . . . . . . . . . . . . . . . Brown 6/0
Head . . . . . . . . . . . . . . . . . . . . . . . Brass bead
Tail . . . . . . . . . . . . . . . . . Pheasant tail fibers
Rib . . . . . . . . . . . . . . . . . . . . . . Copper wire
Body . . . . . . . . . Ringneck pheasant tail fibers,
wrapped herl-style

### Pete's Pheasant Caddis

Hook . . . . . . . . . . . . . . . . . . . TMC 2457; 10-18
Thread . . . . . . . . . . . . . . . . . . . . . . . Black 6/0
Head . . . . . . . . . . . . . . . . . . . . . . . Brass bead
Rib . . . . . . . . . . . . . . . . . . . . . Fine gold wire
Thorax . . . . . . . . . . . . . . . . . . . Peacock herl
Body . . . . . . . . . . . . . . . . . Pheasant tail fibers
Beard . . . . . . . . . . . . Pheasant tail or partridge

### Bead-head Rabbit Emerger

Hook . . . . . . . . . . . . . . . . . . . TMC 2457; 12-16
Thread . . . . . . . . . . . . . . . . . . . . . . . Red 6/0
Head . . . . . . . . . . . . . . . . . . . . . . . Brass bead
Tail . . . . . . . . . . . White Z-lon or Antron yarn
Body . . . . . . . . . . Dark brown rabbit dubbing
Wing . . . . . . . . . . . . . . . . . . . . White calf tail
Thorax . . . . . . . . . Dark brown rabbit dubbing

### Brassie

Hook . . . . . . . . . . . . . . . . . . . TMC 2457; 14-18
Thread . . . . . . . . . . . . . . . . . . . . . . . Black 6/0
Head . . . . . . . . . . . . . . . . . . . . . . Copper bead
Body . . . . . . . . . . . . . . . . . . . . . Copper wire
Thorax . . . . . . . . . . . . . . . . . . . Peacock herl

### Bead-head Serendipity

Hook . . . . . . . . . . . . . . . . . . . TMC 2457; 12-18
Thread . . . . . . . . . . . . . . . . . . . . . . . Red 6/0
Head . . . . . . . . . . . . . . . . . . . . . . . Brass bead
Body . . . . . . Red Z-lon or Antron yarn, twisted
to form a thin strand
Wing . . . . . . . . White deer hair, trimmed short

### Bead-butt Scud

Hook . . . . . . . . . . . . . . . . . . TMC 2457; 8-16
Thread . . . . . . . . . . . . . . . . . . . . Orange 6/0
Tail. . . . . . . . . . . . . . . . . Pheasant-tail fibers
Rib. . . . . . . . . . . . . . . . . . . . . . Amber V-rib
Body . . . . . . . . . . . . Orange Antron dubbing
Shellback. . . . . . . . Clear plastic or pearl Mylar
Butt . . . . Brass bead, slid over tail at hook bend

### Bottle Brush

Hook . . . . . . . . . . . . . . . . . . TMC 2457; 10-16
Thread . . . . . . . . . . . . . . . . . . . . . . Tan 6/0
Head . . . . . . . . . . . . . . . . . . . Copper bead
Tail . . . . . . . . . . . . . . . . . . Two goose biots
Body . . . . . . . . . Natural rabbit hair, twisted with
copper wire or thread
Beard . . . . . . . . . . . . . . . . . . Partridge hackle

### Van's Case Caddis

Hook . . . . . . . . . . . . . . . . . . TMC 2487; 12-18
Thread . . . . . . . . . . . . . . . . . . . . . Olive 6/0
Head . . . . . . . . . . . . . . . . . . . Copper bead
Underbody . . . . . . . Olive hare's mask dubbing
Body . . . . . . . . . Black and yellow Swiss Straw,
clipped randomly
Beard . . . . . . . . . . . . . . . . . . . Partridge hackle
Thorax . . . . . . . . . . Olive hare's mask dubbing

### Theo's Danger Baby

Hook . . . . . . . . . . . . . . . . . . TMC 2457; 8-16
Thread . . . . . . . . . . . . . . . . . . . . . Black 6/0
Head . . . . . . . . . . . . . . . . . . . . Brass bead
Tag. . . . . . . . . . . Fluorescent chartreuse thread
Rib. . . . . . . . . . . . . . . . . . . . Fine gold wire
Body . . . . . . . . . . . . . . . . . . . . Peacock herl
Wing . . . . . . . . . Light olive Z-lon, caddis-style
Thorax . . . . . . . . . . . . . . . . . . . Peacock herl

### Peacock Bead-head

Hook . . . . . . . . . . . . . . . . . . TMC 2457; 12-18
Thread . . . . . . . . . . . . . . . . . . . . . Black 6/0
Head . . . . . . . . . . . . . . . . . . . . Brass bead
Tag . . . . . . . . . . . Fluorescent chartreuse thread
Rib . . . . . . . . . . . . . . . . . . . . Fine gold wire
Body . . . . . . . . . . . . . . . . . . . . Peacock herl

### Gold-bead Possie Nymph

Hook . . . . . . . . . . . . . . . . . . TMC 3761; 8-14
Thread . . . . . . . . . . . . . . . . . . . . . Gray 6/0
Head . . . . . . . . . . . . . . . . . . . . Brass bead
Tail. . . . . . . . . Australian opossum guard hairs
Rib. . . . . . . . . . . . . . . . . . . Fine copper wire
Body . . . . . . . . . . Australian opossum dubbing
Thorax . . . . . . . Australian opossum guard hairs

### Thunderhead

Hook . . . . . . . . . . . . . . . . . . Mustad 9672; 6-12
Thread . . . . . . . . . . . . . . . . . . . . . Black 6/0
Head . . . . . . . . . . . . . . . . . . . Nickel bead
Beard . . . . . . . . . . . . . Chartreuse synthetic hair
or bucktail, tied length of wing
Wing . . . . . . . . . . . . Synthetic hair or bucktail,
purple over black
Rib. . . . . . . . . . . . . . . . . . . Oval gold tinsel
Body . . . . . . . . . . . . . . . . . Flat silver Mylar

### Bead-head Stonefly

Hook . . . . . . . . . . . . . . . . . . Mustad 9672; 4-10
Thread . . . . . . . . . . . . . . . . . . . . Brown 6/0
Head . . . . . . . . . . . . . . . . . . . . Brass bead
Thorax . . . . . . . . . . Brown rabbit dubbing
Hackle . . . . . . . . . . . . . . . . . . . . . Brown
Weight . . . . . . Brass bead, tied in behind thorax
Tail . . . . . . . . . . . . . . . . . . Amber goose biots
Rib . . . . . . . . . . . . . . . . . . . . . Copper wire
Body . . . . . . . . . . . . . . . Brown rabbit dubbing
Wingcase . . . . . . . . . . . Mottled turkey, folded

### Bead-head Giant Black Stonefly

Hook . . . . . . . . . . . . . . . . . . TMC 200R; 2-10
Thread . . . . . . . . . . . . . . . . . . . . . Black 6/0
Head . . . . . . . . . . . . . . . . . . . . Brass bead
Tail. . . . . . . . . . . . . . . . . . Black goose biots
Rib. . . . . . . . . . . . . . . . . . Black Larva Lace
Body . . . . . . . . . . . . . . . Black Antron dubbing
Wingcase . . Black Swiss Straw, folded over thorax
Thorax . . . . . . . . . . . . . . Black Antron dubbing
Legs . . . . . . . . . . Dubbing, plucked from thorax

# Dry Flies

Designed to float on the surface, a dry fly is usually tied on a light-wire hook, and balances on the fibers of its tail and hackle.

Dry flies make up the largest and most diverse category of fly patterns. It includes attractors tied in bright colors; impressionistic searching patterns; and imitators, which mimic the adult forms of various aquatic insects, such as mayflies, caddisflies, midges and stoneflies.

Dry flies are designed primarily for fishing trout, which can be frustratingly selective in their feeding habits. This explains why flytiers have developed hundreds of dry-fly patterns.

When tying a dry fly to match a natural, consider size first. A pattern that is much larger than the natural may spook the fish.

Color is also important. Try to match that of the natural as closely as possible. Some materials, such as dubbing, will change color when they get wet. It's a good idea to choose a body material a few shades lighter than the color of the natural.

POPULAR HOOKS include: (1) TMC 100 and (2) 101; (3) Mustad 94840 and (4) 94842.

Other considerations are durability, buoyancy and visibility to the angler.

Flies made with hair wings and tails float well and stand up to rough water better than those with feather wings and tails.

Treating your flies with floatant helps them stay on the surface longer. Waterproofers (right) can be sprayed on newly tied flies for added flotation.

Flies that float high on the water are easier for the fisherman to see than those in the surface film. For low-riding flies, such as parachutes, use a light-colored or fluorescent wing material. In low-light situations, switch to a light-colored fly.

A favorite dry fly in many situations, the Adams (below and following pages) is a classic searching pattern. Designed in 1922 by Len Halladay for his friend C. F. Adams, it quickly became the most popular dry fly in America, and remains so today.

DRESS flies for slow or clear water (top) more sparsely than flies for rough or dirty water (bottom).

TREAT finished flies with a waterproofer, such as Scotch-guard®, for long-lasting flotation.

*The Adams dry fly*

## How to Tie a Dry Fly: The Adams

| Recipe | |
|---|---|
| Hook . . . . . . . Mustad 94840; 10 - 20 |
| Thread . . . . . . . . . . Gray or black, 6/0 |
| Wing . . . . . . . Grizzly hen-hackle tips |
| Tail . . . . . Brown and grizzly hackle, mixed |
| Body . . . . . . . Medium gray muskrat dubbing |
| Hackle . . . Brown and grizzly, mixed |

### How to Tie an Adams

1 Start thread about one-third shank length behind eye and form a base for tying in wings.

2 Tie in two hackle-point wings as shown on page 64. Wind thread back to hook bend.

3 Strip a small bunch of grizzly hackle fibers, and an equal bunch of brown hackle fibers, for the tail. Stack fibers so tips are aligned.

4 Tie in tail fibers at hook bend. Trim off excess butts and wind thread forward to secure. Wind thread back to bend.

5 Apply a small amount of dubbing to thread. Wind dubbed thread forward.

6 Form a tapered body, leaving a gap between body and wings for tying in and wrapping hackle.

7 Select one grizzly and one brown hackle feather of proper size, and trim webbing from base (p. 67).

8 Tie in hackles with dull side facing you, tips pointing back. Make several turns of thread to secure hackles, and trim butt ends. Wrap thread forward to one hook-eye length behind eye.

9 Grasp tip of first hackle with hackle pliers. Wrap hackle forward, making three wraps behind wing, and three more in front. Secure hackle tip with thread. Repeat with second hackle.

10 Trim excess hackle feathers and any fibers that are trapped under thread turns. Form a head, whip-finish and apply head cement.

# Catalog of Dry Flies

### Adams

| | |
|---|---|
| Hook | Mustad 94840; 10-20 |
| Thread | Black 6/0 |
| Wing | Grizzly hen-hackle tips |
| Tail | Brown and grizzly hackle fibers, mixed |
| Body | Gray muskrat dubbing |
| Hackle | Brown and grizzly, mixed |

### Light Cahill

| | |
|---|---|
| Hook | TMC 100; 10-20 |
| Thread | Cream 6/0 |
| Wing | Lemon wood duck flank fibers |
| Tail | Light ginger hackle fibers |
| Body | Cream dubbing |
| Hackle | Light ginger |

### Light Hendrickson

| | |
|---|---|
| Hook | Mustad 94840; 12-18 |
| Thread | Tan 6/0 |
| Wing | Lemon wood duck flank fibers |
| Tail | Medium blue dun hackle fibers |
| Body | Red fox dubbing |
| Hackle | Medium blue dun |

### Dark Hendrickson

| | |
|---|---|
| Hook | Mustad 94840; 12-18 |
| Thread | Gray 6/0 |
| Wing | Lemon wood duck flank fibers |
| Tail | Dark blue dun hackle fibers |
| Body | Dark gray muskrat dubbing |
| Hackle | Dark blue dun |

### Blue-wing Olive

| | |
|---|---|
| Hook | TMC 100; 12-20 |
| Thread | Olive 6/0 |
| Wing | Blue dun hen-hackle tips |
| Tail | Blue dun hackle fibers |
| Rib | Brown silk thread |
| Body | Medium olive rabbit dubbing |
| Hackle | Blue dun |

### Gray Fox Variant

| | |
|---|---|
| Hook | Mustad 94840; 12-14 |
| Thread | Primrose 6/0 |
| Wing | Mallard flank fibers |
| Tail | Golden ginger hackle fibers |
| Body | Red fox dubbing |
| Hackle | Golden ginger and light grizzly, mixed, oversized |

### Blue Dun

| | |
|---|---|
| Hook | TMC 100; 12-18 |
| Thread | Gray 6/0 |
| Wing | Natural gray duck quill segment |
| Tail | Medium blue dun hackle fibers |
| Body | Gray muskrat dubbing |
| Hackle | Medium blue dun |

### March Brown

| | |
|---|---|
| Hook | Mustad 94840; 10-14 |
| Thread | Brown 6/0 |
| Wing | Turkey quill segment |
| Tail | Dark ginger hackle fibers |
| Rib | Yellow thread or gold oval tinsel |
| Body | Brown rabbit dubbing |
| Hackle | Dark ginger |

### Black Gnat

| | |
|---|---|
| Hook | TMC 100; 12-20 |
| Thread | Black 6/0 |
| Wing | Natural gray duck quill segment |
| Tail | Black hackle fibers |
| Body | Black rabbit dubbing |
| Hackle | Black |

**Mosquito**

| | |
|---|---|
| Hook | TMC 100; 12-18 |
| Thread | Black 6/0 |
| Wing | Grizzly hen-hackle tips |
| Tail | Grizzly hackle fibers |
| Body | Moose mane, quill-style |
| Hackle | Grizzly |

**Red Quill**

| | |
|---|---|
| Hook | Mustad 94840; 12-16 |
| Thread | Gray 6/0 |
| Wing | Lemon wood duck flank fibers |
| Tail | Medium bronze dun hackle fibers |
| Body | Brown hackle stem, quill-style |
| Hackle | Medium bronze dun |

**Quill Gordon**

| | |
|---|---|
| Hook | Mustad 94840; 12-16 |
| Thread | Black 6/0 |
| Wing | Lemon wood duck flank fibers |
| Tail | Dark blue dun hackle fibers |
| Body | Stripped peacock herl |
| Hackle | Dark blue dun |

**Royal Coachman**

| | |
|---|---|
| Hook | Mustad 94840; 10-18 |
| Thread | Black 6/0 |
| Wing | White duck quill segments |
| Tail | Golden pheasant tippet or coachman brown hackle fibers |
| Body | Peacock herl with red floss band |
| Hackle | Coachman brown |

**Renegade**

| | |
|---|---|
| Hook | TMC 100; 6-18 |
| Thread | Black 6/0 |
| Tag | Fine flat gold tinsel |
| Rear Hackle | Brown |
| Body | Peacock herl |
| Front Hackle | White |

**Brown Bivisible**

| | |
|---|---|
| Hook | Mustad 94840; 10-14 |
| Thread | Black 6/0 |
| Tail | Brown hackle fibers |
| Body | Brown hackle, wrapped in tight spirals around rear two-thirds of shank |
| Hackle | Cream |

**Blue Quill**

| | |
|---|---|
| Hook | Mustad 94840; 12-18 |
| Thread | Black 6/0 |
| Wing | Natural gray duck quill segments |
| Tail | Medium blue dun hackle fibers |
| Body | Stripped peacock herl |
| Hackle | Medium blue dun |

**Blue-wing Olive Parachute**

| | |
|---|---|
| Hook | Mustad 94840; 12-20 |
| Thread | Olive 6/0 |
| Wing | Calf body hair, parachute-style |
| Tail | Medium blue dun hackle fibers |
| Body | Olive dubbing |
| Hackle | Medium blue dun |

**Light Cahill Parachute**

| | |
|---|---|
| Hook | TMC 100; 12-18 |
| Thread | Cream 6/0 |
| Wing | Calf body hair, parachute-style |
| Tail | Light ginger hackle fibers |
| Body | Cream dubbing |
| Hackle | Light ginger |

### Pale Morning Dun

```
Hook.....................TMC 100; 12-18
Thread ..........................Cream 6/0
Wing.............Light dun hen-hackle tips
Tail...............Light dun hackle fibers
Body...............Cream rabbit dubbing
Hackle ........................Light dun
```

### Pale Evening Dun

```
Hook ................Mustad 94840; 14-20
Thread ..........................Cream 6/0
Wing ........Light blue dun hen-hackle tips
Tail............Light blue dun hackle fibers
Body ..........Pale yellow rabbit dubbing
Hackle ..................Medium blue dun
```

### Sulphur Dun

```
Hook.....................TMC 100; 16-18
Thread..........................Cream 6/0
Wing..............Cream hen-hackle tips
Tail............Light blue dun hackle fibers
Body..................Cream fox dubbing
Hackle.....................Light blue dun
```

### Borcher Special

```
Hook.................Mustad 94840; 10-18
Thread ..........................Black 6/0
Wing..............Blue dun hen-hackle tips
Tail....Mahogany ringneck pheasant tail fibers
Body........Mottled turkey wing-quill fibers,
                              wrapped herl-style
Hackle ...........Brown and grizzly, mixed
```

### Ginger Fox

```
Hook .....................TMC 100; 12-16
Thread ............................Tan 6/0
Wing ..................Mallard flank fibers
Tail...................Ginger hackle fibers
Underbody................White poly yarn
Body ......................Red fox dubbing
Hackle ...................Golden ginger
```

### Little Marryat

```
Hook................Mustad 94840; 10-18
Thread..........................Cream 6/0
Wing.......Natural gray duck quill segment
Tail...................Brown hackle fibers
Body............Light gray rabbit dubbing
Hackle.............................Brown
```

### Rio Grande King

```
Hook.....................TMC 100; 10-18
Thread ..........................Brown 6/0
Wing..........White duck quill segments
Tail ...............Golden pheasant tippets
Body......................Black chenille
Hackle .............................Brown
```

### Adams Irresistible

```
Hook .................Mustad 94840; 8-14
Thread ..........................Black 3/0
Wing ...........Grizzly hen-hackle tips
Tail......................Moose mane
Body .......Gray deer hair, spun and clipped
Hackle ..........Brown and grizzly, mixed
```

### Royal Humpy

```
Hook.................Mustad 94840; 8-14
Thread..............................Red 6/0
Wing.....White calf body or natural deer hair
Tail...................Natural deer hair
Shellback...............Natural deer hair
Body..............................Red floss
Hackle..............................Brown
```

### Coffin Fly

Hook . . . . . . . . . . . . . . Mustad 94840; 12-14
Thread . . . . . . . . . . . . . . . . . . . . . White 6/0
Wing . . . . . . . . . . . . . . . . . . . . . Teal flank
Tail. . . . . . . . Peccary or moose-mane fibers
Rib. . . . . . . . . . . . . . . . . . . . . White thread
Underbody. . . . . . . . . . . . . . White poly yarn
Body . . . . . . . . White saddle hackle, palmered
over white poly yarn and trimmed
Hackle . . . . . . . . . . . . . Badger-colored hackle

### Western Green Drake

Hook . . . . . . . . . . . . . . . . . . . TMC 100; 10-12
Thread . . . . . . . . . . . . . . . . . . . . . Olive 6/0
Wing . . . . . . . . . . . . . . . . . . Moose body hair
Tail . . . . . . . . . . . . . . . . . . . Moose body hair
Rib . . . . . . . . . . . . . . . . . . . . . . Olive floss
Body . . . . . . . . . . . . . . . . Olive rabbit dubbing
Hackle . . . . . . . . . . . . . . . . . . . Olive grizzly

### Brown Drake

Hook . . . . . . . . . . . . . . . Mustad 94840; 6-16
Thread . . . . . . . . . . . . . . . . . . . . Brown 6/0
Tail. . . . . . . . . . . . . . Brown hackle fibers
Body . . . . . Dark yellow rabbit or poly dubbing
Wing . . . . Dun turkey flats, hackle-point style
Hackle . . . . . . . . . . . . . . . . . . Yellow grizzly

### Moose-mane Adams

Hook . . . . . . . . . . . . . . . . . . . . TMC 100; 8-16
Thread . . . . . . . . . . . . . . . . . . . . . Gray 6/0
Wing . . . . . . . . . . . . . Grizzly hen-hackle tips
Tail. . . . . . . . . . . . . . . . . . . . . Moose mane
Body . . . . . . . . . . . . . . Medium gray dubbing
Hackle . . . . . . . . . . Brown and grizzly, mixed

### White Wulff

Hook. . . . . . . . . . . . . . . Mustad 94840; 6-16
Thread . . . . . . . . . . . . . . . . . . . . . White 6/0
Wing . . . . . . . . . . . . . . . White calf body hair
Tail. . . . . . . . . . . . . . . . White calf body hair
Body . . . . . . . . . . . . . . . White rabbit dubbing
Hackle . . . . . . . . . . . . . . . . Cream or badger

### Gray Wulff

Hook . . . . . . . . . . . . . . . Mustad 94840; 8-14
Thread . . . . . . . . . . . . . . . . . . . . Black 6/0
Wing . . . . . . . . . . . . . Natural brown bucktail
Tail. . . . . . . . . . . . . . Natural brown bucktail
Body . . . . . . . . . . . . . . Gray muskrat dubbing
Hackle . . . . . . . . . . . . . . . Medium blue dun

### Grizzly Wulff

Hook . . . . . . . . . . . . . . . Mustad 94840; 8-14
Thread . . . . . . . . . . . . . . . . . . . . Black 6/0
Wing . . . . . . . . . . . . . Natural brown bucktail
Tail. . . . . . . . . . . . . . Natural brown bucktail
Body . . . . . . . . . . . . . . . . . . . . . Yellow floss
Hackle . . . . . . . . . . Brown and grizzly, mixed

### Royal Wulff

Hook. . . . . . . . . . . . . . . Mustad 94840; 8-14
Thread . . . . . . . . . . . . . . . . . . . . Black 6/0
Wing. . . . . . . . . . . . . . . . . . White calf tail
Tail . . . . . . . . . . . . . . Natural brown bucktail
Body . . . . . . . . . Peacock herl with red floss band
Hackle . . . . . . . . . . . . . . . Coachman brown

### Ausable Wulff

Hook . . . . . . . . . . . . . . . Mustad 94840; 8-14
Thread . . . . . . . . . . . . . . . . . . . . . Red 6/0
Wing . . . . . . . . . . . . . . . White calf body hair
Tail. . . . . . . . . . . . . . . . . . Moose body hair
Body . . . . . . . . . Bleached Australian opossum
Hackle . . . . . . . . . . Brown and grizzly, mixed

### Tent-wing Caddis

Hook . . . . . . . . . . . . . . . . . . . . TMC 100; 12-20
Thread . . . . . . . . . . . . . . . . . . . . . . . . . Tan 6/0
Body . . . . . . . . . . Ringneck pheasant tail fibers, wrapped herl-style
Hackle . . Dark ginger, trimmed top and bottom
Wing . . . . . . Mottled turkey wing-quill segment

### Hemingway Caddis

Hook . . . . . . . . . . . . . . Mustad 94840; 12-20
Thread . . . . . . . . . . . . . . . . . . . . . . . Olive 6/0
Body . . . . . . . . . Medium olive rabbit dubbing
Palmered hackle . . . . . Medium blue dun hackle
Underwing . . . . Lemon wood duck flank fibers
Wing . . . . . . Gray duck quill segment, tent-style
Thorax . . . . . . . . . . . . . . . . . . . . . Peacock herl
Hackle . . . . . . . Medium blue dun, over thorax

### Henryville Special

Hook . . . . . . . . . . . . . . Mustad 94840; 12-20
Thread . . . . . . . . . . . . . . . . . . . . . . . Black 6/0
Body . . . . . . . . . . . . . . . . . . . . . . . Olive floss
Palmered hackle . . . . . . . . . Grizzly, undersized
Underwing . . . . Lemon wood duck flank fibers
Wing . . . . Two natural gray duck quill segments, tent-style
Hackle . . . . . . . . . . . . . . . . . . . . . Dark ginger

### Elk-Hair Caddis

Hook . . . . . . . . . . . . . . . . . . . . TMC 100; 10-20
Thread . . . . . . . . . . . . . . . . . . . . . . . . . Tan 6/0
Body . . . . . . . . . . . . . . . . . . Tan rabbit dubbing
Hackle . . . . . . . . . . . . . . . . Ginger, palmered
Wing . . . . . . . . . . . . . . . . . . . . . . . Tan elk hair

### Peacock Caddis

Hook . . . . . . . . . . . . . . . Mustad 94840; 8-14
Thread . . . . . . . . . . . . . . . . . . . . . . . Black 6/0
Body . . . . . . . . . . . . . . . . . . . . . . Peacock herl
Wing . . . . . . . . . . . . . . . . . . . . . . . Tan elk hair
Hackle . . . . . . . . . . Brown and grizzly, mixed

### Goddard Caddis

Hook . . . . . . . . . . . . . . Mustad 94840; 10-16
Thread . . . . . . . . . . . . . . . . . . . . . . . Black 6/0
Body . . . . . . . . Gray deer hair, spun and clipped
Hackle . . . . . . . . . . . . . . . . . . . . . . . . . Brown
Antennae . . . . . . . . Brown hackle stems, stripped and tied in at head

### Deschutes Caddis

Hook . . . . . . . . . . . . . . . Mustad 94840; 8-12
Thread . . . . . . . . . . . . . . . . . . . . . . . Brown 6/0
Tail . . . . . . . . . . . . . . . . . . . . Natural deer hair
Body . . . . . . . . . Yellow rabbit or poly dubbing
Wing . . . . . . . . . . . . . . . . Light brown deer hair
Hackle . . . . . . . . . . . . . . . . . . . . . Dark ginger

### Delta-wing Caddis

Hook . . . . . . . . . . . . . . Mustad 94840; 10-22
Thread . . . . . . . . . . . . . . . . . . . . . . . . Gray 6/0
Body . . . . . . . . . . . . . . . . . Gray rabbit dubbing
Wing . . . . . . . . . . . . . Blue dun hen-hackle tips
Hackle . . . . . . . . . . . . . . . . . . . . . . Bronze dun

### Small Dun Caddis

Hook . . . . . . . . . . . . . . . . . . . . TMC 101; 16-22
Thread . . . . . . . . . . . . . . . . . . . . . . . . Gray 6/0
Body . . . . . . . . . . . . . . . . . Gray rabbit dubbing
Wing . . . . . . . . . . . . . . . . . . . . . . Mallard flank
Hackle . . . . . . . . . . . . . . . . . . . . . . . . Grizzly

### Slow-water Caddis

Hook . . . . . . . . . . . . . . . . . . TMC 100; 12-20
Thread . . . . . . . . . . . . . . . . . . . . . Olive 6/0
Body . . . . . . . . . . . . . Medium olive dubbing
Hackle . . . . . . . . . . . . . . . . . . . . . . Ginger
Wing . . . . . Dun hen-hackle feathers, lacquered

### King's River

Hook . . . . . . . . . . . . . . . Mustad 94840; 12-18
Thread . . . . . . . . . . . . . . . . . Dark brown 6/0
Body . . . . . . . . . Tannish brown rabbit dubbing
Wing . . . . . Mottled turkey wing-quill segment
Hackle . . . . . . . . . . . . . . . . . . . . . . . Brown

### Rio Grande Trude

Hook . . . . . . . . . . . . . . . Mustad 94840; 10-16
Thread . . . . . . . . . . . . . . . . . . . . Black 6/0
Tail . . . . . . . . . . . . . . Golden pheasant tippet
Body . . . . . . . . . . . . . . Black rabbit dubbing
Wing . . . . . . . . . . . . . . . . . . White calf tail
Hackle . . . . . . . . . . . . . Dark coachman brown

### Little Yellow Stone

Hook . . . . . . . . . . . . . Mustad 94840; 12-16
Thread . . . . . . . . . . . . . . . . . . . . Yellow 6/0
Tail . . . . . . . . . . . . . . . . . Yellow deer hair
Tag . . . . . . . . . . . . . . . . . . . . . Red thread
Palmered hackle . . Ginger, palmered over body
Body . . . . . . . . . . . . . . . . . . . . Yellow floss
Wing . . . . . . . . . . . . . . . . . Yellow deer hair
Hackle . . . . . . . . . . . . . . . . . . . . . . Ginger

### Black Stimulator

Hook . . . . . . . . . . . . . . . . . . TMC 200R; 6-8
Thread . . . . . . . . . . . Fluorescent orange 6/0
Tail . . . . . . . . . . . . . . . . . . . Black elk hair
Rib . . . Fine gold wire and dark blue dun hackle
Body . . . Black goat dubbing; or blend of black,
purple, claret, rust and orange goat
Wing . . . . . . . . . . . Black elk hair, caddis-style
Hackle . . . . . . . . Grizzly, wrapped over thorax
Thorax . . . . . Fluorescent fire-orange dubbing

### Sofa Pillow

Hook . . . . . . . . . . . . . . . . Mustad 9672; 4-10
Thread . . . . . . . . . . . . . . . . . . . . Brown 6/0
Tail . . . . . . . . . . . . . Red goose quill segment
Body . . . . . . . . . . . . . . . . . . . . . Red floss
Wing . . . . . . . . . . . . . Red fox squirrel tail fibers
Hackle . . . . . . . . . . . . . . Brown saddle hackle

### Tan CDC/Elk Caddis

Hook . . . . . . . . . . . . . . . . . . TMC 101; 10-20
Thread . . . . . . . . . . . . . . . . . . . . . Tan 6/0
Rib . . . . . . . . . . . . . . . . . . . Fine gold tinsel
Body . . . . . . . . . . . . . . . . Tan rabbit dubbing
Underwing . . . . . . . . . . . . . . . . . . Tan CDC
Wing . . . . . Elk hair, butts trimmed to form head
Antennae . . . . . . . Stripped ginger hackle stems

### Olive CDC/Elk Caddis

Hook . . . . . . . . . . . . . . . . . . TMC 101; 10-20
Thread . . . . . . . . . . . . . . . . . . . . Olive 6/0
Rib . . . . . . . . . . . . . . . . . . . Fine gold tinsel
Body . . . . . . . . . . . . . . . . Olive rabbit dubbing
Underwing . . . . . . . . . . . . . . . . . Olive CDC
Wing . . . . . Elk hair, butts trimmed to form head
Antenna . . . . . . . . Stripped olive hackle stems

### Gray CDC Caddis

Hook . . . . . . . . . . . . . . . . . . TMC 101; 12-20
Thread . . . . . . . . . . . . . . . . . . . . . Gray 6/0
Tail . . . . . . . . . . . . . Dun hackle fibers, forked
Body . . . . . . . . . . . . . . . Gray muskrat dubbing
Wing . . Gray CDC with two grizzly hackle tips
Sides . . . . . . . . . . . . . . . . . . . . . . Rust CDC

### Cream Midge

Hook . . . . . . . . . . . . . . . . . . . TMC 100; 18-28
Thread . . . . . . . . . . . . . . . . . . . White 6/0
Tail . . . . . . . . . . . . . . . . Cream hackle fibers
Body . . . . . . . . . . . . . . Cream rabbit dubbing
Hackle . . . . . . . . . . . . . . . . . . . . . Cream

### Black Midge

Hook . . . . . . . . . . . . . . . . . . . TMC 100; 20-26
Thread . . . . . . . . . . . . . . . . . . . Black 6/0
Tail . . . . . . . . . . . . . . . . Black hackle fibers
Body . . . . . . . . . . . . . . Black rabbit dubbing
Hackle . . . . . . . . . . . . . . . . . . . . . Black

### Griffith's Gnat

Hook . . . . . . . . . . . . . . Mustad 94840; 18-28
Thread . . . . . . . . . . . . . . . . . . . Olive 6/0
Rib . . . . . . Fine gold wire, wrapped over body
and hackle
Hackle . . . . . Grizzly hackle, palmered over body
Body . . . . . . . . . . . . . . . . . . . Peacock herl

### Trico Spinner

Hook . . . . . . . . . . . . . . . . . . . TMC 100; 20-26
Thread . . . . . . . . . . . . . . . . . . . Black 6/0
Tail . . . . . . . . . . . . . Dun hackle fibers, forked
Body . . . . . . . . . . . . . . . . . . . Black dubbing
Wing . . . . . . . . . . White hen-hackle tips, spent

### Rusty Spinner

Hook . . . . . . . . . . . . . . . . . . . TMC 100; 12-24
Thread . . . . . . . . . . . . . . . . . . . Black 6/0
Tail . . . . . . . . . . . . . Medium dun hackle fibers
Body . . . . . . . . . . Rusty brown rabbit dubbing
Wing . . . . . . Light gray hen-hackle tips, spent

### Red Quill Spinner

Hook . . . . . . . . . . . . . . Mustad 94833; 14-24
Thread . . . . . . . . . . . . . . . . . . . Tan 6/0
Tail . . . . . . . . . . . . . . . . . Brown hackle fibers
Body . . . . . . . . . . Stripped brown hackle stem
Wing . . . . . . . Light dun hen-hackle tips, spent

### Mahogany Dun Thorax

Hook . . . . . . . . . . . . . . . Mustad 94840; 12-16
Thread . . . . . . . . . . . . . . . . . . . Brown 6/0
Tail . . . . . . . . . . . . . . . . Brown hackle fibers
Body . . . . . . . . . . . . Mahogany rabbit dubbing
Wing . . . . . . . . . . . . . . . Blue dun turkey flats,
upright
Hackle . . . . . Brown hackle, clipped on bottom

### Cream Thorax

Hook . . . . . . . . . . . . . . Mustad 94840; 12-20
Thread . . . . . . . . . . . . . . . . . . . Cream 6/0
Tail . . . . . . . . . . . . . . . . Cream hackle fibers
Body . . . . . . . . . . . . . Cream rabbit dubbing
Wing . . . . . . . . . . . . . . . . White turkey flats,
upright
Hackle . . . . . . Cream hackle, clipped on bottom

### Olive Thorax

Hook . . . . . . . . . . . . . . Mustad 94840; 12-20
Thread . . . . . . . . . . . . . . . . . . . Olive 6/0
Tail . . . . . . . . . . . . . . . . Blue dun hackle fibers
Body . . . . . . . . . . . . . . . . . Olive rabbit dubbing
Wing . . . . . . . . . . . . . . . . . . Dun turkey flats,
upright
Hackle . . . . . . . . . Blue dun, clipped on bottom

### Brown No-hackle

Hook . . . . . . . . . . . . . . . . . TMC 5230; 14-20
Thread . . . . . . . . . . . . . . . . . . . . . Brown 6/0
Tail . . . . . . . . . . . Brown hackle fibers, forked
Body . . . . . . . . . . . . . . Brown rabbit dubbing
Wing . . . . . . . . . Dark mallard quill segments

### Olive No-hackle

Hook . . . . . . . . . . . . . . . . . TMC 5230; 14-20
Thread . . . . . . . . . . . . . . . . . . . . . Olive 6/0
Tail . . . . . . . . . Light dun hackle fibers, forked
Body . . . . . . . . . . . . . . . . . . . Olive dubbing
Wing . . . . . . . Natural gray duck quill segments

### Comparadun

Hook . . . . . . . . . . . . . . . Mustad 94840; 14-20
Thread . . . . . . . . . . . . . . . . . . . . . . Tan 6/0
Tail . . . . . . . . . . . . . . . . Brown hackle fibers
Body . . . . . . . . . . . . . . . . . . . . Tan dubbing
Wing . . . . . . . . . . . . . . . Elk or deer body hair

### Goplin Orange Julius

Hook . . . . . . . . . . . . . . . . . Mustad 94840; 12-18
Thread . . . . . . . . . . . . . . . . . . . . . . Cream 6/0
Tail . . . . . . . . . . . . . . . Light dun hackle fibers
Abdomen . . . . . . . . Cream and yellow dubbing
Wing . . . . Cream turkey flat, folded and upright
Thorax . . . . . . . . . . . . . . . . Orange ostrich herl
Hackle . . . . . . . . . . . . . . . . . . . . . . Light dun

### CDC Tailwater Dun

Hook . . . . . . . . . . . . . . . Mustad 94840; 14-20
Thread . . . . . . . . . . . . . . . . . . . . . Olive 6/0
Tail . . . . . . . . . . . . . . . . . Dun hackle fibers
Body . . . . . . . . . . . . . . . . . . . Olive dubbing
Wing . . . . . . . . . . . . . . . . . . . . . Dun CDC
Sides . . . . . . . . . . . . . . . . . . . . . Poly yarn
Thorax . . . . . . . . . . . . . . . . . . . . . . . Olive

### CDC Biot Comparadun

Hook . . . . . . . . . . . . . . . Mustad 94840; 14-20
Thread . . . . . . . . . . . . . . . . . . . . . Gray 6/0
Tail . . . . . . . . . . . . . . . . . Dun hackle fibers
Body . . . . . . . . . . . . . . . . Brown goose biot
Wing . . . . . . . . . . . . . . Mallard flank fibers
Thorax . . . . . . . . . . . . . . . . . . Gray dubbing
Hackle . . . . . . . . . . . . . . . . . . . . Dun CDC

### Peacock Midge

Hook . . . . . . . . . . . . . . . Mustad 94840; 14-18
Thread . . . . . . . . . . . . . . . . . . . . . Black 6/0
Tail . . . . . . . . . . . . Grizzly or red hackle fibers
Body . . . . . . . . . . . . . . . . . . . . Peacock herl
Hackle . . . . . . . . . . . . . . . . . . . . . . Grizzly

### Trico Parachute

Hook . . . . . . . . . . . . . . . . . . TMC 101; 20-24
Thread . . . . . . . . . . . . . . . . . . . . . White 6/0
Tail . . . . . . . . . . . . . . . . Grizzly hackle fibers
Body . . . . . . . . . . . . . . White floss or thread
Wing . . . White hen-hackle tips, parachute-style
Thorax . . . . . . . . . . . . . . Black rabbit dubbing
Hackle . . . . . . . . . Grizzly dun, parachute-style

### Morris May Dark

Hook . . . . . . . . . . . . . . . Mustad 94840; 8-20
Thread . . . . . . . . . . . . . . . . . Dark brown 6/0
Tail . . . . . . . . . . . . . . . . . Ginger hackle fibers
Abdomen . . . . . . . . . . . . . . . Brown poly yarn
Wing . . . . . . . . . . . . . . . . . . Gray poly yarn
Thorax . . . . . . . . . . . . . . Brown poly dubbing
Hackle . . . . . . . . . Brown, wrapped over thorax

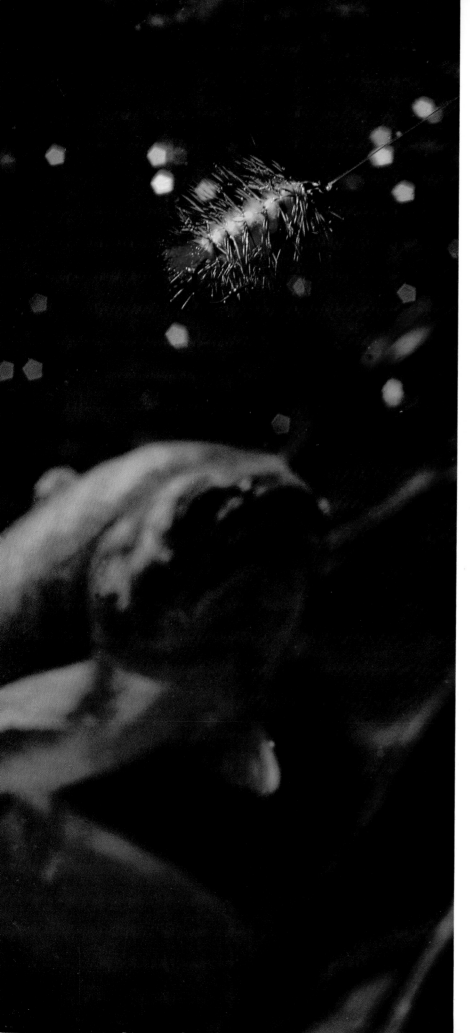

# Wet Flies

A fly angler who took up the sport twenty years ago may never have fished a traditional wet-fly pattern. The fancy patterns of the late 1800s and early 1900s have all but disappeared from most fly shops and catalogs. Yet wet flies were the most popular patterns in America until the 1950s.

Traditional wet flies had colorful names like "Queen of the Waters" and "Wickham's Fancy" and were meant to be fished below the surface to suggest a variety of drowned mayflies. Most were attractor patterns with plenty of flash and color.

Wet flies went out of fashion as more realistic patterns, such as nymphs and dry flies, gained popularity. But wets didn't disappear entirely, and for good reason: they still catch fish.

Today, wet flies are making a comeback. Traditional wet flies like the Parmachene Belle and Wooly Worm (left) remain popular with flytiers and anglers, and the soft-hackle fly, a wet-fly/nymph hybrid developed in England, has found wide acceptance in America.

Though closely related, traditional wet flies and soft-hackle flies differ somewhat in the way they are tied. Wet flies often resemble dry-fly patterns with hackle and wings sloping back over a dubbed body.

POPULAR HOOKS include: (1) TMC 3761; (2) Mustad 3366, (3) 3906 and (4) 7957.

MARRY quill segments of different feathers by stroking edges to interlock barbules, making a multicolor wing.

QUILL-SEGMENT wings for wet flies can be tied in with tips curving up or down to create a different look.

DUB wet-fly bodies to cigar shape. This way, tapered front end allows wings and hackle to slope back.

Soft-hackle flies seldom have wings and are more sparsely tied. They have a tightly dubbed body, and hackle made of partridge, hen or other soft-fibered feathers.

Wet and soft-hackle flies are most effective when fished unweighted on a dead-drift, or as a dropper fly rigged several inches below a dry.

Another type of wet fly is the salmon fly. These complex and beautiful fly patterns are related to both wet flies and streamers, but make up a distinct fly category.

Some salmon flies have elaborate and colorful feather wings. Called *fully dressed*, these patterns rarely see water. They are usually tied for the purpose of display and feature married wings (above). Often made of exotic and hard-to-find materials, fully dressed flies are considered the pinnacle of the flytier's art.

One of the most popular of the traditional wet-fly patterns is the Light Cahill (right, and following pages). It imitates a number of major midseason mayfly species on rivers from Maine to Minnesota.

Created in the 1880s by Dan Cahill, in upstate New York, this fly has a light coloration, making it an ideal pattern for mornings, evenings or any low-light situations. It is also tied in a dry-fly version (p. 96).

*The Light Cahill*

# How to Tie a Wet Fly: The Light Cahill

| **Recipe** |
| --- |
| Hook . . . . . . . . . TMC 3761; 10-16 |
| Thread . . . . . . . . . . . . . . Cream 6/0 |
| Tail . . . Lemon wood duck flank fibers |
| Body . . . . . . . Cream rabbit dubbing |
| Hackle . . . . . . . . . . . . Cream hen or rooster saddle |
| Wing . . . . . . . . . Lemon wood duck flank fibers |

*How to Tie the Light Cahill*

1 Start thread at midpoint of shank and wind back to bend. Strip a small bunch of wood duck flank fibers, or substitute, for tail. Stack fibers so tips are aligned. Length of tail should equal length of hook shank.

2 Tie in tail at hook bend with several soft loops. Trim off excess butt ends.

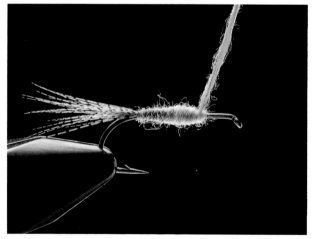

3 Apply a small amount of dubbing to thread and wrap dubbed thread forward to about one-third shank length behind eye.

4 Select a dark cream rooster saddle hackle. Fold hackle by stroking hackle fibers between fingers.

**5** Tie in tip of folded saddle hackle with fibers facing back. Secure with several turns of thread, and trim off excess tip.

**6** Begin winding hackle around shank. Stroke fibers back with fingers after first wrap.

**7** Make two more wraps, and secure hackle stem with several turns of thread. Trim off hackle fibers that lie over top of body so wing will lie flat.

**8** Gather tips of folded wood duck flank feather to make wing. Finished wing should be 1½ times hook-shank length.

**9** Tie in wing on top of hook with several soft loops, and make a few more wraps to secure.

**10** Trim butt end of flank feather. Wrap thread forward and form head. Whip-finish, and apply head cement.

# Catalog of Wet Flies

**Alder**

Hook. . . . . . . . . . . . . . . . . . TMC 3761; 10-14
Thread . . . . . . . . . . . . . . . . . . . . Black 6/0
Tag . . . . . . . . . . . . . . . . Fine flat gold tinsel
Body . . . . . . . . . . . . . . . . . . Peacock herl
Hackle . . . . . . . . . . . . . . . . . . Black hen
Wing. . . . . . . . . Mottled turkey quill segments

**Blue Dun**

Hook . . . . . . . . . . . . . . . . . . TMC 3761; 10-16
Thread . . . . . . . . . . . . . . . . . . . . Gray 6/0
Tail. . . . . . . . . Medium blue dun hackle fibers
Body . . . . . . . . . . . . . . . . Muskrat dubbing
Hackle . . . . . . . . . . Medium blue dun hen
Wing . . . . . . . Natural gray duck quill segments

**Cow Dung**

Hook. . . . . . . . . . . . . . . . . . TMC 3761; 10-16
Thread. . . . . . . . . . . . . . . . . . . . Black 6/0
Tag . . . . . . . . . . . . . . . . Fine flat gold tinsel
Body . . . . . . . . . . . . . . . . . . Dark olive floss
Hackle. . . . . . . . . . . . . . . . . . Brown hen
Wing . . . . . . . . Cinnamon turkey quill segment

**Orvis Light Cahill**

Hook. . . . . . . . . . . . . . . . . . TMC 3761; 10-16
Thread . . . . . . . . . . . . . . . . . . . . Cream 6/0
Tail . . . . . . . . . . . . . . Cream hackle fibers
Body. . . . . . . . . . . . . . . Cream rabbit dubbing
Hackle . . . . . . . . . . . . . . . . . . Cream hen
Wing. . . . . . . . . Lemon wood duck flank fibers

**Dark Cahill**

Hook . . . . . . . . . . . . . . . . . . TMC 3761; 10-16
Thread . . . . . . . . . . . . . . . . . . . . Black 6/0
Tail. . . . . . . . . Lemon wood duck flank fibers
Body . . . . . . . . . . . . . . . . Muskrat dubbing
Hackle . . . . . . . . . . . . . . . . Dark ginger hen
Wing . . . . . . . . Lemon wood duck flank fibers

**Dark Hendrickson**

Hook. . . . . . . . . . . . . . . . . . TMC 3761; 10-16
Thread. . . . . . . . . . . . . . . . . . . . Black 6/0
Tail . . . . . . . . . . . . . . . . Medium blue dun
Body . . . . . . . . . . . . . . . . Muskrat dubbing
Hackle. . . . . . . . . . . . . . Medium blue dun hen
Wing . . . . . . . . Lemon wood duck flank fibers

**Quill Gordon**

Hook. . . . . . . . . . . . . . . . . . TMC 3761; 10-16
Thread . . . . . . . . . . . . . . . . . . . . Black 6/0
Tail . . . . . . . . . Medium blue dun hackle fibers
Body . . . . . . . Stripped peacock stem, quill-style
Hackle . . . . . . . . . . . . . Medium blue dun hen
Wing. . . . . . . . . Lemon wood duck flank fibers

**American March Brown**

Hook . . . . . . . . . . . . . . . . . . TMC 3761; 10-14
Thread . . . . . . . . . . . . . . . . . . . . Black 6/0
Tail. . . . . . . . . . . Mottled grouse hackle fibers
Rib. . . . . . . . . Yellow thread or oval gold tinsel
Body . . . . . . . . . . Grayish tan rabbit dubbing
Hackle . . . . . . . . . . . . . . . . . Mottled grouse
Wing . . . . . . . . Mottled turkey quill segments

**Hornberg**

Hook. . . . . . . . . . . . . . . . . Mustad 9672; 6-10
Thread. . . . . . . . . . . . . . . . . . . . Black 6/0
Body . . . . . . . . . . . . . . . . . Flat silver tinsel
Underwing . . . . . . . . . . . . . . Yellow calf tail
Wing . . . . . . . . . . . Mallard flank feathers,
one on each side
Cheeks . . . . . . . . . . . . . . . . . . . Jungle cock
Hackle. . . . . . . . . . . . . . . . . . . . . Grizzly

### Professor

Hook . . . . . . . . . . . . . . . . . . TMC 3761; 10-16
Thread . . . . . . . . . . . . . . . . . . . . . . Black 6/0
Tail. . . . . . . . . . . . . . . . . . Red hackle fibers
Rib. . . . . . . . . . . . . . . . Fine gold flat tinsel
Body . . . . . . . . . Yellow dubbing or floss
Hackle . . . . . . . . . . . . . . . . . . . Brown hen
Wing . . . . . . . . . . . . . Mallard flank fibers

### Parmachene Belle

Hook. . . . . . . . . . . . . . . . . . TMC 3761; 10-16
Thread . . . . . . . . . . . . . . . . . . . . . . Black 6/0
Tail . . . . . . Red and white hackle fibers, mixed
Rib . . . . . . . . . . . . . . . . Fine gold flat tinsel
Body. . . . . . . . . . . . . . . . . . . . Yellow floss
Hackle . . . . . . . Red hen and white hen, mixed
Wing . . . . . . Married sections of red and white
                                duck quill segments

### Royal Coachman

Hook . . . . . . . . . . . . . . . . . . TMC 3761; 10-16
Thread . . . . . . . . . . . . . . . . . . . . . . Black 6/0
Tail. . . . . . . . . . Golden pheasant tippet fibers
Rib. . . . . . . . . . . . . . . . . . . . Fine gold wire
Body . . . . . . . Peacock herl with red floss band
Hackle . . . . . . . . . . . . . . . . . Dark brown hen
Wing . . . . . . . . . . . White duck quill segments

### Leadwing Coachman

Hook . . . . . . . . . . . . . . . . . . TMC 3761; 6-16
Thread . . . . . . . . . . . . . . . . . . . . . . Black 6/0
Tip . . . . . . . . . . . . . . . . Fine gold flat tinsel
Body . . . . . . . . . . . . . . . . . . . . Peacock herl
Hackle . . . . . . . . . . . . . . . . . . . Brown hen
Wing . . . . . . . Natural gray duck quill segments

### Black Gnat

Hook. . . . . . . . . . . . . . . . . . TMC 3761; 10-14
Thread . . . . . . . . . . . . . . . . . . . . . . Black 6/0
Tail . . . . . . . . . . . . . . . . . . Black hackle fibers
Body . . . . . . . . . . . . . . . Black rabbit dubbing
Hackle . . . . . . . . . . . . . . . . . . . . . Black hen
Wing. . . . . . . . Natural gray duck quill segment

### Pheasant Tail

Hook . . . . . . . . . . . . . . . . . . TMC 3761; 10-16
Thread . . . . . . . . . . . . . . . . . . . . . Olive 6/0
Rib. . . . . . . . . . . . . . . . . . Fine copper wire
Body . . . Pheasant tail fibers, wrapped herl-style
Hackle . . . . . . . . . . . . . . . . . Brown partridge

### Partridge and Yellow

Hook . . . . . . . . . . . . . . . . . . TMC 3761; 10-16
Thread. . . . . . . . . . . . . . . . . . . . . Yellow 6/0
Abdomen. . . . . . . . . . . . . . . . . . . Yellow floss
Thorax. . . . . . . . . . . . . Natural rabbit dubbing
Hackle . . . . . . Brown partridge or mallard flank

### Tup's Indispensable

Hook. . . . . . . . . . . . . . . . . . TMC 3761; 10-16
Thread . . . . . . . . . . . . . . . . . . . . . Yellow 6/0
Tail . . . . . . . . . . . . . Blue dun hen-hackle fibers
Body. . . . . . . . . . . . . . . . . . . . . Yellow floss
Thorax . . . . . . . . . . . Light pink rabbit dubbing
Hackle . . . . . . . . . . . . . . . . . . . Blue dun hen

### Yellow Wooly Worm

Hook . . . . . . . . . . . . . . . . . . . TMC 3761; 2-12
Thread . . . . . . . . . . . . . . . . . . . . . . Black 6/0
Tail. . . . . . . . . . . . . . . . . . Red hackle fibers
Rib. . . . . . . . . . . . . . . . . . . Fine silver wire
Body . . . . . . . . . . . . . . . . . . Yellow chenille
Hackle . . . . . . . . . . . . . . . Grizzly, palmered

## Rusty Rat

| | |
|---|---|
| Hook | TMC 7999; 2-10 |
| Thread | Red 6/0 |
| Tag | Fine gold oval tinsel |
| Tail | Peacock sword fibers |
| Rib | Gold oval tinsel |
| Body | Rear half, yellow floss; front half, peacock herl |
| Wing | Gray fox guard hair |
| Cheeks | Jungle cock (optional) |
| Hackle | Grizzly |

## Cosseboom

| | |
|---|---|
| Hook | TMC 7999; 2-10 |
| Thread | Red 6/0 |
| Tag | Silver flat tinsel |
| Tail | Medium olive floss |
| Rib | Silver flat tinsel |
| Body | Medium olive floss |
| Wing | Gray squirrel tail |
| Hackle | Lemon yellow |

## Hairy Mary

| | |
|---|---|
| Hook | Mustad 36890; 4-10 |
| Thread | Black 6/0 |
| Tag | Gold oval tinsel |
| Tail | Golden pheasant crest |
| Rib | Gold oval tinsel |
| Body | Black floss |
| Beard | Bright blue hackle fibers |
| Wing | Brown fitch (fur) tail fibers |

## Red Abbey

| | |
|---|---|
| Hook | Mustad 36890; 4-10 |
| Thread | Black 6/0 |
| Head | Black or Red |
| Tag | Silver oval tinsel |
| Tail | Red goose quill segment or bucktail |
| Rib | Silver flat or oval tinsel |
| Body | Red floss or wool yarn |
| Beard | Brown hackle, pulled down |
| Wing | Light brown squirrel tail hair, or brown bucktail |
| Cheeks | Jungle cock (optional) |

## Black Dose

| | |
|---|---|
| Hook | Mustad 36890; 4-10 |
| Thread | Black 6/0 |
| Tag | Silver oval tinsel |
| Butt | Pale yellow floss |
| Tail | Golden pheasant crest, covered half its length by red hackle fibers |
| Rib | Silver oval tinsel |
| Body | Black floss |
| Wing | Four peacock sword fibers, and bundle of black bear fibers |
| Beard | Black hen hackle |
| Cheeks | Jungle cock (optional) |

## Undertaker

| | |
|---|---|
| Hook | TMC 7999; 2-10 |
| Thread | Black 6/0 |
| Tag | Fine gold flat tinsel |
| Butt | Rear half, fluorescent green floss; front half, fluorescent orange floss |
| Rib | Gold oval tinsel |
| Body | Peacock herl |
| Beard | Black hackle |
| Wing | Black bear hair |

## Jock Scott

Hook . . . . . . . . . . . . . . . . . . . . . . . . . . . . . . . . . . . . . . TMC 7999; 5/0-6
Thread . . . . . . . . . . . . . . . . . . . . . . . . . . . . . . . . . . . . . . . . . Black 6/0
Tag. . . . . . . . . . . . . . . . . . . . . . . . . . Flat silver tinsel and yellow floss
Tail. . . Golden pheasant crest, covered half its length with orange hackle
Butt . . . . . . . . . . . . . . . . . . . . . . . . . . . . . . . . . . . . Black ostrich herl
Body . . . . . . . Rear half, yellow silk floss ribbed with small silver tinsel; front half, black silk floss ribbed with medium silver tinsel; toucan, tied in above and below hook at midpoint of shank
Hackle . . . . . . . . . . . . . . . Black hackle over black floss section of body
Beard . . . . . . . . . . . . . . . . . . . . . . . . . . Gallina or black hen hackle
Wing . . . . Two strips of black turkey with white tips, golden pheasant tail, bustard, gray mallard, peacock sword fibers, blue swan, yellow and red macaw, bronze mallard
Topping . . . . . . . . . . . . . . . . . . . . . . . . . . . . Golden pheasant crest
Sides . . . . . . . . . . . . . . . . . . . . . . . . . . . . . . . . . . . . Jungle cock
Cheeks. . . . . . . . . . . . . . . . . . . . . . Blue chatterer and blue macaw

## Black Doctor

Hook . . . . . . . . . . . . . . . . . . . . . . . . . . . . . . . . . . . . TMC 7999; 5/0-6
Thread . . . . . . . . . . . . . . . . . . . . . . . . . . . . . . . . . . . . . . Black 6/0
Tag. . . . . . . . . . . . . . . . . . . . . . . . . . . . Silver thread, yellow floss
Tail. . . . . . . . . . . . . . . . . . . . . . Golden pheasant crest and Indian crow
Butt . . . . . . . . . . . . . . . . . . . . . . . . . . . . . . . . . . . . Scarlet wool
Body . . . . . . . . . . . . . . . . . . . . . . . . . . . . . . . . . . . . Black floss
Rib. . . . . . . . . . . . . . . . . . . . . . . . . . . . . . . . . . Silver oval tinsel
Hackle . . . . . . . . . . . . . . . . . . . . . . . . . . . . . . . . . Dark claret
Beard. . . . . . . . . . . . . . . . . . . . . . . . . . . Speckled gallina or hen
Wing . . . . . . . . . Golden pheasant tippet and crest strands; peacock wing; married strands of scarlet, blue and yellow swan, florican bustard; light mottled turkey tail; married strips of teal and narrow strips of brown mallard
Topping . . . . . . . . . . . . . . . . . . . . . . . . . . . . Golden pheasant crest
Head. . . . . . . . . . . . . . . . . . . . . . . . . . . . . . . . . . . . Scarlet wool

## Gordon

Hook . . . . . . . . . . . . . . . . . . . . . . . . . . . . . . . . . . . TMC 7999; 5/0-6
Thread . . . . . . . . . . . . . . . . . . . . . . . . . . . . . . . . . . . . . Black 6/0
Tag. . . . . . . . . . . . . . . . . . . . . . . . . Flat silver tinsel and yellow floss
Tail. . . . . . . . . . . . . . . . . . . . . Golden pheasant crest and tippet
Butt . . . . . . . . . . . . . . . . . . . . . . . . . . . . . . . . Black ostrich herl
Body . . . . . . . . Rear one-third, yellow floss; front two-thirds, claret floss
Rib. . . . . . . . . . . . . . . . . . Silver oval tinsel and silver flat tinsel
Hackle . . . . . . . . . . . . . . . Claret hackle, palmered over claret floss
Beard. . . . . . . . . . . . . . . . . . . . . . . . . . . . . . . . . Blue hackle
Wing . . . . . Pair of golden pheasant sword feathers; yellow, blue and red swan; bustard; Lady Amherst pheasant tail
Topping . . . . . . . . . . . . . . . . . . . . . . . . . . . . Golden pheasant crest
Cheeks. . . . . . . . . . . . . . . . . . . . . . . . . . . . . . . . . Jungle cock

# Terrestrials

But don't be afraid to try a terrestrial pattern in early and late season as well. Terrestrials such as ants and beetles are a staple in a trout's diet throughout the season, and their imitations can be used as searching patterns when no insects are emerging.

Even during a heavy mayfly hatch, some trout will rise to terrestrials that drift into their feeding window.

Cast a terrestrial along the bank or shoreline. Twitch it occasionally to make it look like a struggling insect. This will draw fish from farther away than will a fly drifting motionless.

Success with terrestrial imitations isn't limited to trout fishing. Panfish and bass will readily take a hopper or cricket pattern twitched on the surface of a lake or farm pond.

When the hot summer winds blow across the water, trout feed heavily on the increasing numbers of land insects, or *terrestrials*, that accidently fall, or are blown into, lakes and streams. Then, a well-tied terrestrial imitation can be extremely productive.

## How to Make Legs for Hoppers and Crickets

**1** Select two large hackle feathers.

**2** Trim off ends of fibers, leaving ⅛-inch stubs along stem.

**3** Tie an overhand knot in middle of stem to form leg joint. Crimp stem ⅛ inch from end to form foot.

## Tips for Tying Terrestrials

POPULAR HOOKS include: (1) Mustad 94840; (2) TMC 101; (3) Mustad 94833, and (4) 9671; (5) TMC 100 and (6) Mustad 9672.

ADD a small piece of fluorescent yarn, or *indicator,* to the top of a terrestrial pattern so you can see it more easily.

Terrestrial types include:

*Ants.* These small insects make up a large percentage of the natural terrestrials that find their way into the water. Trout feed on ants whenever they are available, making imitations effective from early spring through late fall.

*Hoppers and Crickets.* Although they represent only a small percentage of a fish's diet, hoppers and crickets are commonly taken by trout, panfish and bass, especially in late summer. Many terrestrial patterns are tied complete with legs (above).

*Beetles.* The opportunistic trout will rise to a beetle even in winter, making beetle imitations year-round producers. Imitations are tied using deer hair or foam bodies, often with a small piece of fluorescent yarn (above).

One of the most effective terrestrial patterns is the Deer-hair Beetle (below, and following pages). Tied with dyed deer hair over a body of peacock herl, this pattern is easy to tie, floats well and consistently catches fish all season long.

*The Deer-hair Beetle*

# How to Tie a Terrestrial: The Deer-hair Beetle

| Recipe | |
|---|---|
| Hook . . . . . . | Mustad 94840; 10 - 16 |
| Thread . . . . . . . . . . . . . . . | Black 3/0 |
| Shellback . . . . . . . . | Black deer hair |
| Body . . . . . . . . . . . . . | Peacock herl |

## How to Tie the Deer-hair Beetle

1 Start thread at middle of hook shank.

2 Snip a small bundle of deer hair, about the diameter of a pencil.

3 Hold deer hair by tips, and comb out short underfur with dubbing needle.

4 Tie in butt ends of deer hair at middle of hook shank, with tips facing back. Don't be concerned if butts flare slightly; wind thread over them to secure.

5 Trim any excess butts, then wind thread back to hook bend.

6 Tie in two or three strands of herl and trim butt ends. Wind thread forward to 1/8 inch behind eye.

7 Wrap herl forward around shank and secure with several turns of thread. Trim excess herl.

8 Bring tips of deer hair forward over herl and tie in just behind eye to form *shellback*. Make several firm wraps with thread, and whip-finish.

9 Trim off excess tips to form head of beetle.

10 Snip one or two strands from each side of rear of body to form legs. Apply head cement.

# Catalog of Terrestrials

## Black Fur Ant

Hook. . . . . . . . . . . . . . . . . . . TMC 100; 14-20
Thread . . . . . . . . . . . . . . . . . . . . . . Black 6/0
Abdomen . . . . . . . . . . . . Black rabbit dubbing
Hackle . . . . . . . . . . . . . . . . . . . . . . . . . Black
Thorax . . . . . . . . . . . . . Black rabbit dubbing

## Foam Ant

Hook . . . . . . . . . . . . . . . . . . . TMC 100; 14-20
Thread . . . . . . . . . . . . . . . . . . . . . . Black 6/0
Abdomen. . . . . . . . . . . . . . . . . . Black foam
Hackle . . . . . . . . . . . . . . . . . . . CDC feathers
Indicator . . . . . . . . . . . . . . . . . Yellow foam
Legs. . . . . . . . . . . . . . . . . Black Krystal Flash
Thorax . . . . . . . . . . . . . . . . . . . . Black foam
Antennae . . . . . . . . . . . . Black Krystal Flash

## Flying Ant

Hook. . . . . . . . . . . . . . . . . . . TMC 100; 14-18
Thread. . . . . . . . . . . . . . . . . . . . . . Black 6/0
Abdomen . . . . . . . . . . . . Black rabbit dubbing
Wing . . . . . . . . Mallard quill segment, tent-style
Legs . . . . . . . . . . . . . . . . . Moose-mane fibers
Hackle. . . . . . . . . . . . . . . . . . . . Black hackle
Thorax . . . . . . . . . . . . . Black rabbit dubbing

## Black Beetle

Hook. . . . . . . . . . . . . . . . . . . TMC 100; 14-20
Thread . . . . . . . . . . . . . . . . . . . . . . Black 6/0
Shellback . . . . . . . Black deer hair, pulled over
body and clipped to form legs and head
Body. . . . . . . Black wool yarn or peacock herl

## Foam Cricket

Hook . . . . . . . . . . . . . . . . . . . TMC 100; 8-14
Thread . . . . . . . . . . . . . . . . . . . . . . Black 6/0
Abdomen. . . . . . . . . . . . . . . . . . Black foam
Thorax . . . . . . . . . . . . . . . . Foam tied at eye
Legs. . . . Black goose biots and black Krystal Flash
Antennae . . . . . . . . . . . . . Black Krystal Flash

## CDC Peacock Beetle

Hook. . . . . . . . . . . . . . . . . . . TMC 100; 14-16
Thread. . . . . . . . . . . . . . . . . . . . . . Black 6/0
Shellback . . . . . . . . . . . . . Black CDC feathers
Body. . . . . . . . . . . . . . . . . . . . . Peacock herl
Legs . . . . . . . . . . . . . . . . Black CDC feathers
Head . . . . . . . . . Butts from shellback, trimmed

## Dave's Cricket

Hook. . . . . . . . . . . . . . . . . Mustad 94833; 6-12
Thread . . . . . . . . . . . . . . . . . . . . . . Black 6/0
Tail . . . . . . . . . Black deer hair and brown yarn
Body. . . . . . . . . . . . . . . . . . . . . . Brown yarn
Hackle . . . . Black hackle, palmered and clipped
Wing. . . . Black goose quill segment, tent-style
Legs . . . . . . . . . . . Black hackle stems, trimmed
and knotted
Collar . . . . . . . . . . . . . . . . . . . Black deer hair
Head . . . . . . . Black deer hair, spun and clipped

## Henry's Fork Cricket

Hook . . . . . . . . . . . . . . . . . Mustad 94833; 6-16
Thread . . . . . . . . . . . . . . . . . . . . . Brown 6/0
Body . . . . . . . . . . . . . . . . . . . Brown deer hair
Wing . . . . . . . . . . Black hen saddle, lacquered
Head . . . . . . Black elk hair, tied with tips facing
forward, then pulled back
Legs. . . . . . . . . . . . . . . . Black rubber, knotted

## Green Leaf Hopper

Hook. . . . . . . . . . . . . . . . . . . TMC 100; 16-22
Thread. . . . . . . . . . . . . . . . . . . . . . White 6/0
Body . . . . . . . . . . . . . . . . . . . . . . White thread
Hackle. . . . . Insect green hackle, palmered over
body, clipped top and bottom
Wing . . . . Insect green mallard flank, lacquered

### Letort Hopper

Hook . . . . . . . . . . . . . . . . Mustad 94833; 8-16
Thread . . . . . . . . . . . . . . . . . . . . . . . Gray 6/0
Body . . . . . . . . . . . . . Yellow rabbit dubbing
Wing . . . . . . . . . . Mottled turkey quill segment
Overwing . . . . . . . . . . . . . . . Natural deer hair
Head . . . . . Natural deer hair, spun and clipped

### Rubber Legs Henry's Fork Hopper

Hook . . . . . . . . . . . . . . . . Mustad 94833; 8-12
Thread . . . . . . . . . . . . . . . . . . . . . Yellow 6/0
Body . . . . . . . . . . . . . . . . . White deer hair
Rib . . . . . . . . . . . . . . . . . . . . Yellow thread
Underwing . . . . . . . . . . . . . . . Yellow elk hair
Wing . . . . . . . . Speckled hen saddle, lacquered
Head . . . Elk hair, tied in with tips facing forward,
          then pulled back to form head and collar
Legs . . . . . . . . . . Rubber leg material, knotted

### Joe's Hopper

Hook . . . . . . . . . . . . . . . . Mustad 94833; 6-14
Thread . . . . . . . . . . . . . . . . . . . . . Black 6/0
Tail . . . . . . . . . . . . . . . . . . Red hackle fibers
Butt and body . . . . . . . . . . . Yellow poly foam
Palmered hackle . . . . . . . Brown hackle, clipped
Wings . . . . . . . . . Mottled turkey quill segment
Hackle . . . . . . . . . . . Brown and grizzly, mixed

### Dave's Hopper

Hook . . . . . . . . . . . . . . . . . Mustad 94833; 4-12
Thread . . . . . . . . . . . . . . . . . . . . . . . Gray 6/0
Tail . . . . . . . . . . Red deer hair and yellow yarn
Body . . . . . . . . . . . . . . . . . . . . . Yellow yarn
Hackle . . . . . . . . . Brown, palmered and clipped
Underwing . . . . . . . . . . . . . . . . Yellow calf tail
Wing . . . Turkey wing-quill segment, lacquered
Legs . . . . . . . . . . . Yellow grizzly hackle stems,
                          clipped and knotted
Collar . . . . . . . . . . . . . . Natural deer hair, spun
Head . . . . . . Natural deer hair, spun and clipped

### Jan's Hopper

Hook . . . . . . . . . . . . . . . . Mustad 94833; 6-16
Thread . . . . . . . . . . . . . . . . . . . . . Black 6/0
Tail . . . . . . . . Red hackle fibers, with a loop of
                   yellow wool yarn
Body . . . . . . . . . . . . . . . . . Yellow wool yarn
Rib . . . . . . . . . . . Brown hackle, trimmed short
Wing . . . . . . . . . . . . . . . . . . . . . Tan elk hair
Hackle . . . . . . . . . . . Brown and grizzly, mixed

### Parachute Hopper

Hook . . . . . . . . . . . . . . . . Mustad 94833; 8-14
Thread . . . . . . . . . . . . . . . . . . . . . . . Tan 6/0
Wing post . . . . . White calf body, parachute-style
Body . . . . . . . . . . . . . . . . . Tan rabbit dubbing
Tent wing . . . . . . Mottled turkey quill segment
Legs . . . . Ringneck pheasant tail fibers, knotted
Hackle . . . . . . . . . . . . . . Grizzly, parachute-style

### Jassid

Hook . . . . . . . . . . . . . . . . . . TMC 101; 16-24
Thread . . . . . . . . . . . . . . . . . . . . . Black 6/0
Body . . . . . . . . . . . . . . . . . . . . . Black thread
Hackle . . . . . . . . . Ginger, palmered over body,
                       trimmed on bottom
Wing . . . . . . . . . . . . Single jungle cock feather

### Inchworm

Hook . . . . . . . . . . . . . . . . Mustad 94840; 10-14
Thread . . . . . . . . . . . . . . . . . . . . . . Green 3/0
Body . . Green bucktail, tied in at eye, extending
         back over bend, with thread wrapped
         open spiral over entire length
Indicator . . . . . . . . . . . . . . . . . Fire orange yarn

### Caterpillar

Hook . . . . . . . . . . . . . . . . . . Mustad 9672; 6-8
Thread . . . . . . . . . . . . . . . . . . . . . . Black 3/0
Rear hackle . . . . . . . . . . . . . . . . . . . . . Grizzly
Rib . . . . . . . . . . . . . . . . . . . . . . . . Silver wire
Overbody . . . . . . Peacock herl, tied in over back
Body . . . . . . . . . . . . . . . . . . . . . . . Yellow floss
Front hackle . . . . . . . . . . . . . . . . . . . . . Grizzly

# Bass & Pike Flies

Anglers across the country are discovering the thrill of catching bass, pike and even muskie on big artificial flies.

Most bass and pike flies imitate some kind of aquatic foods, such as minnows, frogs, crayfish, mice, leeches, worms and, occasionally, large insects. Other patterns rely on flash, color and noise to provoke an aggressive response.

The keys to tying effective bass and pike patterns are size, color and action.

SIZE. Select a fly suitable for the size fish you are after. Smallmouth bass generally prefer 2- to 3-inch flies; largemouth, 3- to 5- inch. Pike and muskie, which often pursue baitfish one-fourth their own length, will often take a fly up to ten inches.

COLOR. In general, flies for clear water should be more subdued than those for murky water. But many fly fishermen prefer white or yellow for surface flies; blues and violets for subsurface. Don't be afraid to experiment with a variety of color combinations to find one that works best for you.

ACTION. Spun deer hair can be trimmed to produce a popping or gurgling sound when retrieved with a quick, short, stripping action. Surface patterns are often tied with lifelike legs and tails to imitate mice, frogs or other aquatic foods.

Other patterns are designed to dive below the surface when retrieved, mimicking a struggling or injured

POPULAR HOOKS include: (1) Mustad 3399; (2) 79666, a weedless keel hook; (3) TMC 800S, and (4) mustad 37187.

POPULAR THREADS include: (1) 2/0 Danville Plus, (2) 3/0 Monocord and (3) superstrong 1/0 Kevlar.

minnow. Subsurface patterns are often tied with long tails made of marabou, rabbit strips, hackle feathers or synthetic hair that pulses like fins or gills under water.

Some patterns, such as the Dahlberg Diver (below, and following pages), are designed to do both.

*The Dahlberg Diver*

MAKE a weedguard from a 4-inch length of piano wire. Bend and crimp wire as shown, and tie in at eye after wrapping body materials so crimp covers point.

## How to Tie a Bass Fly: The Dahlberg Diver

| Recipe | |
|---|---|
| Hook | TMC 800S; 2-10 |
| Thread | White 3/0 |
| Weedguard | Heavy clear mono |
| Wings | Red saddle-hackle feathers |
| Tail | Red deer hair |
| Collar | Red deer hair |
| Head | Red deer hair, spun and clipped |

*How to Tie the Dahlberg Diver*

1 Start thread at hook bend and wrap down to middle of bend. Cut a 5-inch length of heavy clear monofilament for weedguard. Tie in one end of monofilament.

2 Select, size and prepare six saddle hackles for wings. Tie in three on each side of shank at hook bend. Hackle feathers should flare outward.

3 Snip and prepare a clump of deer body hair. Align tips in stacker.

4 Position clump of deer hair over shank directly in front of wings with tips facing back.

5 Make several soft loops to secure. Do not allow tips of deer hair to flare. Place finger against back side of hair while cinching to prevent it from spinning. Tips will form tail.

6 Tie in and spin second clump of hair directly in front of first. Continue adding, spinning and packing hair until shank is covered. Leave about ⅛-inch gap behind eye. Whip-finish, and trim off excess thread.

7 Turn the hook upside down in vise. Trim bottom of fly with scissors or razor blade so it is flat and level. Cut as close as possible to shank, taking care not to cut thread wraps.

8 Turn the hook right side up. Trim front half of deer hair body to bullet shape, as shown, with tips of scissors. Leave a collar of flared deer hair behind tapered head.

9 Trim ends of collar to approximately twice the radius of the body.

10 Reattach thread at hook eye. Push monofilament up through eye and fold back over head of fly. Secure with several turns of thread. Trim off butt end of mono, and whip-finish.

# Catalog of Bass & Pike Flies

## Deer-hair Bug

Hook . . . . . . . . . . . . . . . . . . . . . . . . . . . . . . . . . . . . TMC 800S; 4-10
Thread . . . . . . . . . . . . . . . . . . . . . . . . . . . . . . . . . . . . . . . Olive 3/0
Weedguard . . . . . . . . . . . . . . . . . . Heavy clear monofilament (optional)
Tail . . . . . . . . . . . Yellow marabou, red and pearl Krystal Flash and two
orange grizzly saddles, each side
Sides . . . . . . . . . . . . . . . . . . Orange hackle, red Krystal Flash, each side
Legs . . . . . . . . . . . . . . . Orange rubber, pearl and red Krystal Flash
Head . . . . . . . . . . . . . . . . . Various colors of deer hair, spun and clipped
Eyes . . . . . . . . . . . . . . . . . . . . . . . Plastic doll eyes, glued to head

## Krazy Kicker Frog

Hook . . . . . . . . . . . . . . . . . . . . . . . . . . . . . . . . . . Mustad 3366; 2-10
Thread . . . . . . . . . . . . . . . . . . . . . . . . . . . . . . . . . . . . . . Olive 3/0
Legs . . . . . Light green bucktail, tied one-fourth shank length from bend,
bucktail wrapped with thread to form joint
Body . . . . . . . . . Light green and dark green deer hair, spun and clipped
Weedguard . . . . . . . . . . . . . . . . . . . . . . . . . . Heavy clear monofilament

## Clouser Minnow

Hook . . . . . . . . . . . . . . . . . . . . . . . . . . . . . . . . . TMC 800S; 1/0-6
Thread . . . . . . . . . . . . . . . . . . . . . . . . . . . . . . . . . . . . . . Brown 3/0
Eyes . . . . . . . . . . . . . . . Hourglass eyes, painted red with black pupils
Beard . . . . . . . . . . . . . . . . . . . . . . . . . . . . . . . Orange bucktail
Wing . . . . . . . . . . . . . . . . . . . . Red bucktail, with copper Krystal Flash

## Dave's Crayfish

Hook (upside down) . . . . . . . . . . . . . . . . . . . . . . . . . . . TMC 300; 1/0-8
Thread . . . . . . . . . . . . . . . . . . . . . . . . . . . . . . . . . . . . . Orange 3/0
Eyes . . . . . . . . . . . . . . . . . . . . . . . . . . . . . . . . . . . . Monofilament
Antennae . . . . . . . . . . . . . . . . . . . . . . . . . Two dark moose body fibers
Pincers . . . . . . . . . . . . . . . . . . . . . . . . . . . Orange speckled hen
Rib . . . . . . . . . . . . . . . . . . . . . . . . . . . . . . . . . . . . . . Copper wire
Hackle . . . . . . . . . . . . . . . . . . . . . . . . . . . . . Orange grizzly hackle
Body . . . . . . . Burnt orange Antron yarn, picked out with dubbing needle
Shellback . . . . . . . Orange Swiss Straw, with black waterproof markings

## Rabbit Clouser

Hook . . . . . . . . . . . . . . . . . . . . . . . . . . . . . TMC 800S; 1/0-6
Thread . . . . . . . . . . . . . . . . . . . . . . . . . . . . . . . . . . . . . . Yellow 3/0
Body . . . . . . Red and yellow rabbit strips, glued to shank top and bottom
Legs . . . . . . . . . . . . . . Yellow rubber legs, pearl and red Krystal Flash
Eyes . . . . . . . . . . . . . . . . . . . . . . . . . . . . . Nickel hourglass eyes
Weedguard . . . . . . . . . . . . . . . . . . Heavy clear monofilament (optional)

## Nix's Sunfish

Hook . . . . . . . . . . . . . . . . . . . . . . . . . . . . . . . . . TMC 8089; 1/0-6
Thread . . . . . . . . . . . . . . . . . . . . . . . . . . . . . . . . . . . . . . White 3/0
Weedguard . . . . . . . . . . . . . . . . . . Heavy clear monofilament (optional)
Rib . . . . . . . . . . . . . . . . . . . . . . . . . . . . . . . . . . . . . . Copper wire
Body . . . . . . . . . . . . . . . . . . . . . . . . . Green rabbit or Antron dubbing
Tail and Fins . . . . . . . . Green grizzly hen saddle, tied down with ribbing
Sides . . . . . . . . . . . . . . . . . . . . . . . . . . . . . . . Red hen-hackle tips
Head . . . . . . . . . . Green wool dubbing, with orange wool on underside,
trimmed to shape
Eyes . . . . . . . . . . . . . . . . . . . . . . . . . . . Plastic doll eyes, glued to head

## Dahlberg's Mega Diver

| | |
|---|---|
| Hook | TMC 800S; 2/0-4 |
| Thread | Chartreuse 3/0 |
| Wing | Chartreuse synthetic hair with strands of gold Flashabou |
| Collar and head | Chartreuse deer hair, spun and clipped |
| Weedguard | Piano wire, bent to shape |
| Eyes | Plastic doll eyes, glued to head |

## Whitlock's Hairwater Pup

| | |
|---|---|
| Hook | Mustad 36890; 2-10 |
| Thread | Purple 3/0 |
| Weedguard | Heavy clear monofilament |
| Tail | Purple rabbit fur strip |
| Rib | Fine silver wire |
| Body | Purple rabbit dubbing |
| Beard | Purple Flashabou |
| Collar | Purple deer hair |
| Head | Purple deer hair, spun and clipped |
| Eyes | Purple doll eyes |

## Mouserat

| | |
|---|---|
| Hook | Mustad 37187; 2-10 |
| Thread | Black 3/0 |
| Weedguard | Heavy clear monofilament |
| Tail | Dark brown suede strip |
| Body | Dark deer hair, spun |
| Ears | Dark brown suede, cut to shape |
| Collar | Dark deer hair, spun |
| Head | Dark deer hair, spun and clipped |
| Whiskers | Dark moose body hair |
| Eyes | Black waterproof marker |

## Chamois Leech

| | |
|---|---|
| Hook | TMC 7999; 1/0-6 |
| Thread | Green 6/0 |
| Weedguard | Heavy clear monofilament |
| Butt | Fluorescent orange yarn |
| Rib | Fine copper wire |
| Underbody | Brown Antron dubbing, picked out with dubbing needle |
| Body | Olive chamois strip over back of entire fly, left long to form tail and colored with green and black marker |
| Hackle | Brown speckled hen saddle |
| Eyes | Silver bead-chain |

### Dahlberg Rabbit Strip Diver

Hook. . . . . . . . . . . . . . . . . . . . . . . . . . . . . . . . Mustad 37187; 2-10
Thread . . . . . . . . . . . . . . . . . . . . . . . . . . . . . . . . . . . . White 3/0
Weedguard . . . . . . . . . . . . . . . . . . . . . . Heavy clear monofilament
Tail . . . . . . . . . . . . . . . . . . . . . . . . . . . . . Yellow rabbit fur strip

Topping . . . . . . . . . . . . . . . . . . . . . . . . . . . . . . . Gold Flashabou
Collar . . . . . . . . . . . . . . . . Yellow deer hair, spun and clipped to shape
Head. . . . . . . . . . . . . . . . . . . . . Yellow deer hair, spun and clipped

### Dahlberg Skipper

Hook. . . . . . . . . . . . . . . . . . . . . . . . . . . . . . . . TMC 800S; 2-6
Thread . . . . . . . . . . . . . . . . . . . . . . . . . . . . . . . . . . . White 3/0
Tail . . . . . . . . . . . . . . . . . White synthetic hair, with pearl Mylar
Sides. . . . . . . . . . . . . . . . . . . . . . . . . . . . . . . . . . Red marabou
Collar and Head . . . . . . . . . . . . . . White deer hair, spun and clipped
Weedguard . . . . . . . . . . . . . . . . . . . . . . Piano wire, bent to shape
Eyes . . . . . . . . . . . . . . . . . . . . . . . . . . . . . Yellow doll eyes

### Dahlberg Diving Bug

Hook . . . . . . . . . . . . . . . . . . . . . . . . . . . . . . . TMC 800S; 2-10
Thread . . . . . . . . . . . . . . . . . . . . . . . . . . . . . . . . . . . White 3/0
Weedguard. . . . . . . . . . . . . . . . . . . . . Heavy clear monofilament
Wing. . . . . . . . . . . . . . . . . . . . . . . . . . . . . . . . . . Black marabou
Sides. . . . . . . . . . Two grizzly hackles, with pearl Mylar and peacock herl
Collar . . . . . . . . . . . . . . . . . . . . . . . . . . . . . . . . . Black deer hair
Head. . . . . . . . . . . . . . . . . . . . . Black deer hair, spun and clipped

### Murray's Strymph

Hook. . . . . . . . . . . . . . . . . . . . . . . . . . . . . . . . TMC 5263; 2-10
Thread . . . . . . . . . . . . . . . . . . . . . . . . . . . . . . . . . . . Black 3/0
Tail . . . . . . . . . . . . . . . . . . . . . . . . . . . . . . Black ostrich herl
Body. . . . . . . . . . . . . . . . . . . . . . . . Black rabbit, thickly dubbed
Hackle . . . . . . . . . . . . . . . . . . . . . . . . . . . . . Brown hen saddle

### Green Bomber

Hook . . . . . . . . . . . . . . . . . . . . . . . . . . . . . . . . TMC 7999; 2-8
Thread . . . . . . . . . . . . . . . . . . . . . . . . . . . . . . . . . . . Black 3/0
Tail . . . . . . . . . . . . . . . . . . . . . . . . . . . . . . . . . . White calf tail
Palmered hackle. . . . . . . . . . . . . Brown hackle, palmered through body
Body. . . . . . . . . . . . . . . . . . . . . . Green deer hair, spun and clipped
Wing. . . . . . . . . . . . . . . . . . . . White calf tail, upright-and-divided
Hackle . . . . . . . . . . . . . . . . . . . . . . . . . . . Brown, dry-fly style

## Barr's Bouface

| | | | |
|---|---|---|---|
| Hook . . . . . . . . . . . . . . . . . . . . . . . . . . . . . . . . TMC 800S; 1/0-4 | Tail . . . . . . . . . . . . . . . Black rabbit strip, with Mylar and Krystal Flash |
| Thread . . . . . . . . . . . . . . . . . . . . . . . . . . . . . . . . . . . . Black 3/0 | Body . . . . . . . . . . . . . . . . . . . Black marabou on top, with yellow below |

## Eelworm

| | |
|---|---|
| Hook . . . . . . . . . . . . . . . . . . . . . . . . . . . . . TMC 7999; 1/0-6 | Body . . . . . . . . . . . . . . . . . . . . . . . . . . . . . . . . . . . Black wool yarn |
| Thread . . . . . . . . . . . . . . . . . . . . . . . . . . . . . . . . . . . . . Red 3/0 | Hackle . . . . . . . . . . . . . . . . . . . . . . . . . . . . Black, palmered over body |
| Weedguard . . . . . . . . . . . . . . . . . . . . . Heavy clear monofilament | Eyes . . . . . . . . . . . . . . . . . . . . . . . . . . . . . . . . . Large silver bead-chain |
| Tail . . . . . . . . . . . . . . . . . . . . . . . . . Four black saddle-hackle feathers | |

## Whitlock's Hair Worm

| | |
|---|---|
| Hook . . . . . . . . . . . . . . . . . . . . . . . . . . . . . . TMC 8089; 2-10 | Tail . . . . . . . . . . . . . . . . . . . . . . Six-inch blue rabbit strip, tied in at eye |
| Thread . . . . . . . . . . . . . . . . . . . . . . . . . . . . . . . . . . . . White 3/0 | Body . . . . . . . . . . . . . . . . . Blue rabbit strip, glued to shank and tail strip |
| Weedguard . . . . . . . . . . . . . . . . . . . . . Heavy clear monofilament | Eyes . . . . . . . . . . . . . . . . . . . . . . . . . . . . . . . . . . . . . . White doll eyes |

# Saltwater Fly Patterns

In the last twenty-five years, fly fishing in saltwater has exploded in popularity. Saltwater gamefish are amazingly diverse and range in size from redfish, snook, stripers and bonefish to tarpon, tuna, and marlin. With a seemingly endless supply of saltwater fly-fishing destinations, fly anglers are hitting the coasts and blue water from the arctic to the equatorial waters. And as the sport of saltwater fly fishing grows, so does the range and diversity of saltwater fly tying.

Advances and innovations in synthetic materials have led to the development of non-traditional fly patterns designed specifically for saltwater gamefish.

Types of saltwater patterns include:

*Simple Minnows and Baitfish*—Perhaps the most common, universal and productive patterns are those that imitate the basic elements of a saltwater predator gamefish's diet. Among these baitfish are anchovies, alewives, mackerel, herring, ballyhoo, silversides, and needlefish.

*Tarpon Flies*—The prize of the warm coastal waters from Nova Scotia to Brazil and the coast of Africa, the tarpon is one of the toughest-fighting of the saltwater gamefish. Flies tied to catch tarpon mimic the slender needlefish that make up the tarpon's diet. Sharp hooks are an essential part of any tarpon pattern.

*Crustaceans*—Shrimp and crab patterns are deadly from the Northeast clear to the Gulf of Mexico and beyond. Worked along the shallow bottom of estuarine waters, crustaceans will produce strikes even when little else will.

SHARPEN your hook with a file before you begin tying on material. This will prevent damaging the finished fly.

*Poppers*—Most anglers agree that the aggressive surface strikes of any gamefish ranks among the biggest thrills in fishing. Like their freshwater counterparts, saltwater poppers imitate a struggling baitfish, and few hungry gamefish can resist them. Applying a shiny material, such as aluminum duct tape, to a simple foam popper body can create an amazingly productive saltwater pattern.

One of the most popular saltwater fly patterns is the Whistler, developed by Dan Blanton. The Whistler's dense hackle and bead-chain eyes create a vibration in the water, making it particularly useful in roiled or murky water. It is simple to tie and extremely effective in almost all coastal waters and conditions.

*The Whistler Saltwater Fly*

REMOVE the copper core from a short length of electrical cord. Slip the remaining plastic sheath over the sharpened tip of the hook up to the barb. This will help prevent nicking your thread or your fingers while tying the fly.

## How to Tie a Saltwater Fly: The Whistler

| Recipe | |
| --- | --- |
| Hook | TMC 600SP |
| Size | 4/0–1/0 |
| Thread | Red 3/0 |
| Weight | Lead wire |
| Eyes | Large stainless bead chain |
| Tail | White bucktail with several strands of silver Flashabou or Krystal Flash |
| Sides | Red Saddle Hackle |
| Body | Red Crystal Chenille |
| Collar | Red saddle or neck hackle, densely wrapped |

*How to Tie the Whistler*

1 Start thread at hook bend and wrap forward to just behind hook eye. Wrap lead wire around hook shank. Wrap thread back over lead and forward to just behind hook eye.

2 Attach bead chain eyes with several figure-eight turns of thread. Wind thread back to hook bend.

3 Cut small bundle of white bucktail. Comb out underfur with dubbing needle. Stack bucktail fibers to align tips.

4 Tie in bucktail with several soft loops. Add strands of Flashabou or Krystal Flash. Trim butt ends.

5 Attach sides of red saddle hackle with tips aligned and curving in. Trim excess material.

6 Tie in length of red Crystal Chenille and make several wraps around hook shank. Secure and trim excess.

7 Tie in two strands of red saddle or neck hackle. Wind thread forward to just behind bead chain eyes.

8 Wrap first saddle hackle around hook shank to just behind bead chain eyes and secure.

9 Wrap second hackle forward, palmering hackle to form a dense collar. Secure and trim butt ends.

10 Pass thread in front of bead chain eyes. Form a neat head. Secure with several whip finish knots and trim excess thread. Add head cement and allow to dry.

# Catalog of Saltwater Flies

## Bigeye Tarpon

Hook. . . . . . . . . . . . . . . . . . . . . . . . . . . . . . . . . . . . . . . . TMC 600SP
Size. . . . . . . . . . . . . . . . . . . . . . . . . . . . . . . . . . . . . . . . . . . 4/0 – 1
Thread . . . . . . . . . . . . . . . . . . . . . . . . . . . . . . . . . . . . . . . . . Red 3/0
Weight . . . . . . . . . . . . . . . . . . . . . . . . . . . . . . .Lead wire (optional)
Tail . . . . . . . . . Two black-and-white grizzly saddle hackle and two
red-and-black grizzly saddle hackle feathers
Collar . . . . . . . . . . . One black-and-white grizzly saddle hackle and one
red-and-black grizzly saddle hackle feathers, densely wrapped
Body. . . . . . . . . . . . . . . . . . . Red tying thread, tied in tarpon-body style
Eyes . . . . . . . . . . . . . . . . . . . . . . . . . . . . . .Black and white painted

## Crazy Charley

Hook. . . . . . . . . . . . . . . . . . . . . . . . . . . . . . . . . . . . . . . . TMC 811S
Size. . . . . . . . . . . . . . . . . . . . . . . . . . . . . . . . . . . . . . . . . . . . . . 2-8
Thread . . . . . . . . . . . . . . . . . . . . . . . . . . . . . . . . . . . . . . . . 3/0 White
Eyes . . . . . . . . . . . . . . . . . . . . . . . . . . . . Stainless Bead Chain
Tail . . . . . . . . . . . . . . . . . . . . . . . . . . . . . . . .Pearl Krystal Flash
Body. . . . . . . . . . . . . . . . . . . . . . . . . . Clear V-Rib over pearl tinsel
Wing. . . . . . . . . . . . . . . . . . . . . . . . . . . . . . . . . . .White calf tail

## Bendback Deceiver

Hook. . . . . . . . . . . . . . . . . . . . . . . . . . . . . . . . . . . . . . . . TMC 8115
Size. . . . . . . . . . . . . . . . . . . . . . . . . . . . . . . . . . . . . . . . . . . 2–4/0
Thread . . . . . . . . . . . . . . . . . . . . . . . . . . . . . . . . . . . . . . . White
Wing. . . . . . . . . . . . . . . . . .White saddle hackle with several strands
of silver Flashabou and peacock herl
Collar . . . . . . . . . . . . . . . . . . . . . . . . . . . . . . . . . White bucktail
Eyes . . . . . . . . . . . . . . . . . . . . . . . . . . . . . . . . . . Doll eyes

## Bonefish Special

Hook. . . . . . . . . . . . . . . . . . . . . . . . . . . . . . . . . . . . . . . . TMC 800S
Size. . . . . . . . . . . . . . . . . . . . . . . . . . . . . . . . . . . . . . . . . . . 2 - 8
Thread . . . . . . . . . . . . . . . . . . . . . . . . . . . . Black 6/0 or 3/0
Tail . . . . . . . . . . . . . . . . . . . . . . . . . . . . . . . . . . .Orange marabou
Body. . . . . . . . . . . . . . . . . . . .Clear mono or v-rib over gold Mylar tinsel
Wing. . . . . . . . . . . . . . . . . . . . . . . . .White calftail and crystal flash
Sides. . . . . . . . . . . . . . . . . . . . . . . . . . Grizzly hackle tip on each side
Head . . . . . . . . . . . . . . . . . . . . . . . . . . . Built up and tapered thread

## 'Cuda Fly

Hook. . . . . . . . . . . . . . . . . . . . . . . . . . . . . . . . . .Owner AKI
Size. . . . . . . . . . . . . . . . . . . . . . . . . . . . . . . . . . . . . .2/0 - 4
Thread . . . . . . . . . . . . . . . . . . . . . . . . . . .Fluorescent green 3/0
Tail/Body . . . . . . . . . . . . . . . . . . . . .Fluorescent green Mylar tubing

Collar . . . . . . . . . . . . . . . . . . . . . . . . . . . .Butt ends of tubing flared out
Head . . . . . . . . . . . . . . . . . . . . . . . . . . .Fluorescent green tying thread
Eyes . . . . . . . . . . . . . . . . . . . . .Holographic stick-on coated with epoxy

## Cockroach

Hook . . . . . . . . . . . . . . . . . . . . . . . . . . . . . . . . . . . . . . . . TMC 600SP
Size . . . . . . . . . . . . . . . . . . . . . . . . . . . . . . . . . . . . . . . . . 4/0 – 2
Thread . . . . . . . . . . . . . . . . . . . . . . . . . . . . . . . . . . . . . . Black 3/0
Tail . . . . . . . . . . . . . . . . . . . . . . . . . . . . . . . . Grizzly saddle hackle
Collar . . . . . . . . . . . . . . . . . . . . . . . . . . . . . . . . . . . . Brown bucktail
Body . . . . . . . . . . . . . . . Black tying thread wrapped tarpon-body style
Eyes . . . . . . . . . . . . . Prismatic stick-on or painted, coated with epoxy

## Gotcha

Hook . . . . . . . . . . . . . . . . . . . . . . . . . . . . . . . . . . . . . . . . . TMC 811S
Size . . . . . . . . . . . . . . . . . . . . . . . . . . . . . . . . . . . . . . . . . . . 2-8
Thread . . . . . . . . . . . . . . . . . . . . . . . . . . . . . . . . . . . . . . Pink 3/0
Eyes . . . . . . . . . . . . . . . . . . . . . . . . . . . . . . . Stainless Bead Chain
Tail . . . . . . . . . . . . . . . . . . . . . . . . . . . . . . . . . Pearl Krystal Flash
Body . . . . . . . . . . . . . . . . . . . . . . . . . . . Peral braided Mylar tinsel
Wing . . . . . . . . . . . . . . . . . . . . . . . . . . . . Tan wing fiber or craft fur
Head . . . . . . . . . . . . . . . . . . . . . . . . . . . . . . . . . . . Pink tying thread

## Carpet Crab

Hook . . . . . . . . . . . . . . . . . . . . . . . . . . . . . . . . . . . . . . . . . TMC 811S
Size . . . . . . . . . . . . . . . . . . . . . . . . . . . . . . . . . . . . . . . . . 1/0-6
Thread . . . . . . . . . . . . . . . . . . . . . . . . . . . . . . . . . . . . Brown 3/0
Eyes . . . . . . . . . . . . . . . . . . . . . . . . . . . . . . . . . . . . . . . Dumbbell
Claws . . . . . . . . . . . . . . . . . . . . Tan marabou and grizzly neck hackle
Body . . . . . . . . . . . . . . . . . . . . Strands of tan and brown stiff rug yarn,
available at craft stores for hooking rugs
Legs . . . . . . . . . . . . . . . . . . . . . Cream rubber legs knotted and barred
with brown marker, if desired

## Pad Crab

Hook . . . . . . . . . . . . . . . . . . . . . . . . . . . . . . . . . . . . . . . . . TMC 811S
Size . . . . . . . . . . . . . . . . . . . . . . . . . . . . . . . . . . . . . . . . . 1/0-6
Thread . . . . . . . . . . . . . . . . . . . . . . . . . . . . . . . . . Chartreuse 3/0
Eyes . . . . . . . . . . . . . . . . . . . . . . . . . . . . . . . . . . . . . . . Dumbbell
Claws . . . . . . . . . . . . . . . . . . . . Tan marabou and grizzly neck hackle
Body . . . . . . . . . . . . . . . . . . . . Adhesive pad, colored olive or tan
Legs . . . . . . . . . . . . . . . . . . . . . Cream rubber legs knotted and barred
with brown marker, if desired

## Mantis Shrimp

Hook. . . . . . . . . . . . . . . . . . . . . . . . . . . . . . . . . . . . . . . . . . Gamakatsu SS15
Size. . . . . . . . . . . . . . . . . . . . . . . . . . . . . . . . . . . . . . . . . . . . . . . . . 2 - 8
Thread . . . . . . . . . . . . . . . . . . . . . . . . . . . . . . . . . . . . . . . . . . . Tan 3/0
Eyes . . . . . . . . . . . Burned mono tied in facing backward at hook bend
Tail . . . . . . . . . . . . . . . . . . . . . . . Pumpkin/Black Fleck Sili Legs
Body. . . . . . . . . . . . . . . . . . . . . . . . . . . . . Dubbed tan Craft Fir
Eyes . . . . . . . . . . . . . . . . . . . . . . . . . . Silver medium bead chain
Head. . . . . . . . . . . . . . . . . . . . . . . . . . . . Dubbed tan craft fir

## Soft Foam Popper

Hook. . . . . . . . . . . . . . . . . . . . . . . . . . . . . . . . . . . . . . . . . . . . . TMC 911S
Size. . . . . . . . . . . . . . . . . . . . . . . . . . . . . . . . . . . . . . . . . . . . . . 2/0-8
Thread . . . . . . . . . . . . . . . . . . . . . . . . . . . . . . . . . . . . . . . . . . Unwaxed
Tail . . . . . . . . . . . . . . . . . . . . . . . . . . . . . . . Bucktail and Flashabou
Body. . . . . . . . . . . . . . . . . . . . . . . . . . . . . . . . . Pre-made foam body
Eyes . . . . . . . . . . . . . . . . . . . . . . . . . . . . . . Doll eyes with stems

## Seaducer

Hook. . . . . . . . . . . . . . . . . . . . . . . . . . . . . . . . . . . . . . . . . . . TMC 811S
Size. . . . . . . . . . . . . . . . . . . . . . . . . . . . . . . . . . . . . . . . . . . . 2/0-6
Thread . . . . . . . . . . . . . . . . . . . . . . . . . . . . . . . . . . . . . . . . Red 3/0
Tail . . . . . . . . . . . . . . . . . . . White neck hackle with several strands
of silver Krystal Flash
Body. . . . . . . . . . . . . . . White saddle hackle, wrapped over hook shank
Collar . . . . . . . . . . . . . . . . . . . . . . . . . . . . . Red saddle hackle

## Sand Eel

Hook. . . . . . . . . . . . . . . . . . . . . . . . . . . . . . . . . . . . . . . . . . . TMC 811S
Size. . . . . . . . . . . . . . . . . . . . . . . . . . . . . . . . . . . . . . . . . . . . 2/0-2
Thread . . . . . . . . . . . . . . . . . . . . . . . . . . . . . . . . . . . . . . . . Gray 3/0
Tail . . . . . . . . . . . . . . White and olive Super Hair with silver Lite-Brite,
measured four hook-shank lengths
Body. . . . . Silver braided Mylar. Color top with green permanent marker
Eyes . . . . . . . . . . . . . . . . . . . . . . . . . . . . . . . . . . . . . . . . . Red 3D
Head. . . . . . . . . . . . . . . . . . . . . . . . . . . . . . . . . . . . . . . . . . Epoxy

# Index

# Creative Publishing international
## Your Complete Source of How-to Information for the Outdoors

**Hunting Books**
- Advanced Turkey Hunting
- Advanced Whitetail Hunting
- Black Bear Hunting
- Bowhunting Equipment & Skills
- Bowhunter's Guide to Accurate Shooting
- The Complete Guide to Hunting
- Dog Training
- Elk Hunting
- How to Think Like a Survivor
- Hunting Record-Book Bucks
- Mule Deer Hunting
- Muzzleloading
- Outdoor Guide to Using Your GPS
- Pronghorn Hunting
- Waterfowl Hunting
- Whitetail Hunting
- Whitetail Techniques & Tactics
- Wild Turkey

**Fishing Books**
- Advanced Bass Fishing
- The Art of Freshwater Fishing
- The Complete Guide to Freshwater Fishing

- Fishing for Catfish
- Fishing Rivers & Streams
- Fishing Tips & Tricks
- Fishing with Artificial Lures
- Inshore Salt Water Fishing
- Kids Gone Campin'
- Kids Gone Fishin'
- Largemouth Bass
- Live Bait Fishing
- Modern Methods of Ice Fishing
- Northern Pike & Muskie
- Offshore Salt Water Fishing
- Panfish
- Salt Water Fishing Tactics
- Smallmouth Bass
- Striped Bass Fishing: Salt Water Strategies
- Successful Walleye Fishing
- Trout
- Ultralight Fishing

**Fly Fishing Books**
- The Art of Fly Tying
- The Art of Fly Tying – CD-ROM
- Complete Photo Guide to Fly Fishing

- Complete Photo Guide to Fly Tying
- Fishing Dry Flies
- Fishing Nymphs, Wet Flies & Streamers
- Fly-Fishing Equipment & Skills
- Fly Fishing for Beginners
- Fly Fishing for Trout in Streams
- Fly-Tying Techniques & Patterns

**Cookbooks**
- All-Time Favorite Game Bird Recipes
- America's Favorite Fish Recipes
- America's Favorite Wild Game Recipes
- Backyard Grilling
- Cooking Wild in Kate's Camp
- Cooking Wild in Kate's Kitchen
- Dressing & Cooking Wild Game
- The New Cleaning & Cooking Fish
- Preparing Fish & Wild Game
- The Saltwater Cookbook
- Venison Cookery
- The Wild Butcher

To purchase these or other Creative Publishing international titles,
contact your local bookseller, or visit our website at
www.creativepub.com

The Complete
FLY FISHERMAN™